Also written by Eleanor Hammond;

My First Tarot Deck Limited Edition – ISBN 978-0-9872989-0-4
My First Tarot Deck – ISBN 978-0-9872989-2-8
Take Back Your Soul; Shamanic soul retrieval – ISBN 978-0-646-48034-3

My First Tarot Course

IN-DEPTH TRAINING, EXERCISES, AND QUESTIONS AND ANSWERS TO TEST YOUR KNOWLEDGE.

Eleanor Hammond

BALBOA.
PRESS
A DIVISION OF HAY HOUSE

Balboa Press books may be ordered through booksellers or by contacting:

Balboa Press
A Division of Hay House
1663 Liberty Drive
Bloomington, IN 47403
www.balboapress.com.au
1 (877) 407-4847

ISBN: 978-1-4525-2429-0 (sc)
ISBN: 978-1-4525-2432-0 (e)

Printed in the United States of America.

Balboa Press rev. date: 10/13/2014

With Thanks...

Firstly, thank you to everyone connected to me spiritually over the years. Working with you has been an honor and this course book has been designed to enable my teaching to continue after I'm gone.

Thank you to those people who worked with this book prior to publication. You've given me feedback from the student's perspective which has helped me create something of value.

Special thanks to Tara East and Kym Anderson for editing the book for me. It's hard to be a good friend and give criticism and feedback and I thank you both for doing so.

Thank you to my family who gave me the space to do the work that I love and to my husband Ken who supports me in everything that I do. Love you, babe.

Gratitude to everyone embarking on this journey with me. You are continuing a course of study that has survived centuries.

Blessings to you,
Eleanor

Contents

Introduction

You do not need the tarot deck that I created in order to learn from this book. This book holds the same teaching which can be applied to any and all tarot decks. A tarot deck has seventy-eight standard card meanings and is different from an Oracle deck which could have any number of cards with different meanings across decks.

This book is written to help people who have no understanding of the tarot to become professional tarot readers and it has been written in an easy to understand way, with real students being taken through this process to ensure that all questions that may come up are actually answered within the book.

The whole purpose of the book is to help you to come to an understanding of what tarot means to **you** and how to put it into your own life context.

Within this manual you will be finding out that you have already been through each circumstance described within the tarot, and when you identify each of the seventy-eight meanings to your own life, then you will see how easy it is to read the cards.

Everyone that opens this book will be at various stages of tarot learning, this book is designed for everyone as it will give a basic understanding to those people who don't know about tarot at all, and it will deepen the knowledge of anyone that does.

For instance, there are seventy-eight cards in a tarot deck, and The Fool is considered the first card of the deck. It depicts the soul's journey starting. We have been The Fool many times in our life - when we have our first baby, and when we are the baby, as it's a whole new lifetime that we are beginning. We are The Fool when we fall in love, start a business, or school. We're The Fool when we start every single thing that we start. The Fool relates to the beginning of every undertaking – whether physical, emotional or spiritual.

You would be right in thinking 'I'm there now - it's a new beginning, a new learning, a new journey for me, with this book.'

You are taking the risk of opening your mind to something new and I congratulate you on this. It can be daunting to learn something new.

The Fool is often depicted by a person dancing along, completely oblivious to the rest of his world and environment. They dance next to a cliff with a dog nipping at their heels. They're looking up and don't have any idea where they're going.

So we are foolish in all sorts of different ways, and as soon as you use the word fool, people automatically assume you mean foolish.

No. The Fool is the very first step in any endeavor.

Maslow created this learning pattern below to show the stages that people move through when they learn something new, and why learning might be considered stressful when not taken one step at a time. I have used this pattern throughout this book to ensure that I take you through the learning process in a way that will ensure that you are proficient in tarot by the end.

Maslow's stages of competence:

1. Blissful ignorance / Unconscious Incompetence (The Fool tarot card)
2. I need to learn something? / Conscious Incompetence
3. I can do it, but I'm still learning / Conscious Competence
4. I can do it without thinking about it! / Unconscious Competence!

We all start from **unconscious incompetence**. "I don't know what I don't know yet". This is a very easy state to be living in, as when we are unaware that we don't know everything, we're relaxed. If we had no idea there was an earth quake coming, we'd sit down, have a cup of tea, and read our book, without a care in the world. Even if you already think you know everything within the tarot before you opened this book, you still might learn something you didn't previously know.

Consider how a teenager might feel when he's told he can learn how to drive now.

• He doesn't know what he doesn't know.

And then we come into the next stage; **conscious incompetence**. At this stage we can be made aware of a gap in our knowledge that we didn't even know we had. This stage can be stressful. There's a lot of pedals and levers to learn.

• He knows, that he doesn't know, how to drive.

And then, after practice, we move into **conscious competence** where we know how to do a reading with the tarot cards and we understand all the cards, but we need to refer back to the manual all the time. This stage can be considered the deep learning stage and therefore can feel mentally draining. Don't worry though! We are going to take our time! In this stage the teenager who is learning to drive a car, now knows how to use the pedals and levers, but has to think about every single move before he makes it.

• He knows what he needs to know, but has to think before making each move.

Then we move into **unconscious competence** where everything is now really easy and we are doing things without thinking about them. We'll have the cards on the table and it will be like our intuition is doing the reading for us. Another example of conscious competence is driving a car and going on a trip and, on arrival, not recalling the journey; you drove all that way without thinking about it

- We know what we are doing and don't have to think about it.

Most of our lives are in the unconscious competence space, that's where we feel comfortable and we as human beings don't like getting out of that comfortable zone.

Every time we start something new we go right back to the beginning, right back to unconscious incompetence. Even if you know the tarot, you still might find information in this book that you didn't realize you were missing. You didn't know you didn't know it.

People can sit in unconscious competence for years and not realize it. For instance there's someone who has worked in a job for twenty years and a new employee starts. The first person has been doing their job for twenty years and feels very competent. The new person takes a look around and says "hey did you realize you didn't have to pick this up, you can wait until it gets to here, and it will fall sideways onto a neat pile?"

All of a sudden the person who was in unconscious competence falls straight into conscious incompetence and it's hard for them; with the added burden that they feel like a twit for not seeing the obvious. "I didn't know that I didn't know that!"

If you have never touched a tarot card before then you may be thinking; there are seventy-eight of these cards and I don't know any of them.

This is when all sorts of fears can kick in:

- How is Eleanor going to help me to learn all of this? I won't remember.
- How long is this going to take?
- Do I have time?

The obvious answer of course is that there is always enough time, however the true answer is that we will be moving through this course in a structured way which will allow you to remember the tarot meanings through repetition.

Please trust me, as I understand the way that you will learn and I am here not just to teach you seventy-eight cards, but to teach you the most fundamental and basic ideas around the use of any tarot deck.

You will enter the unconscious competence stage where the cards fall on the table and all of a sudden you are relating things and it's just so easy. This just takes time. We have enough time and I will walk you through step by step.

Here goes?

CHAPTER ONE

Brief Background of the Tarot

You do not have to remember all of the facts below. Just read the information and know that we will move through everything in more depth later in the book. This part of the book gives you the basics around how the tarot was created.

I am talking about tarot cards throughout this book, not oracle cards. There is a difference.

Tarot decks always have seventy-eight cards, and all seventy-eight have the exact same meaning, just interpreted in different ways. The basic principles are always the same. Oracle decks are different from deck to deck. Some oracle decks are about animals, or fairies, or dolphins, for instance, whereas all tarot decks are related to humans and human existence and growth.

Occasionally an author will create a seventy-eight card tarot deck and then add an extra card as a wild card – an unlimited potential card. For instance, I own a deck which has a seventy-ninth card called the unlimited potential card.

This is a tarot deck that doesn't have seventy-eight cards in it:

This probably looks very familiar to most people.

Lots of people use tarot cards without realizing it, and I have met many people that say that they've never been brave enough to use tarot cards, and yet they play poker with friends. The fifty-two card playing deck is actually a tarot deck.

Now we consider the five elements split up against the fifty-two playing card deck. (You don't need to remember this now; just read on.)

- Earth: diamonds, the precious gem we find in the earth. Everything that feeds us comes from the earth.
- Air: Spade comes from the Italian word for sword, which cuts through the air.
- Fire: A Club is wood, and wood burns.
- Water: The heart holds the emotions; tears of joy and sadness.
- There is no Spirit suit in the fifty-two-card playing deck.

The fifty-two-card playing deck has the above four suits of cards. Each suit has thirteen cards, from one (ace) to ten and jack, queen, and king.

The jack, queen, and king were added around the 15th century, as royalty didn't appreciate having a reading when there were cards that were appropriate for every man. Royalty wanted their own cards, and this was at a time when the boy in the family was the prince and girls were considered less important. Therefore, the jack, was added to indicate the child of royalty – jack (child), queen, and king.

As time went on, it became important for the royals to show a difference between their sons and daughters, and the prince card was born - the jack becoming the princess. The court cards becoming the princess (jack), the prince (new), and the queen and king.

The major change to the tarot deck was the inclusion of the Spirit suit. Awareness of spirituality meant that people wanted to describe our soul's journey in this lifetime and beyond, and therefore the twenty-two cards were created to describe the soul's journey on earth.

The spirit suit, or Major Arcana, major secrets, or soul secrets suit was added as people developed spiritually. People wanted to understand where they were on their soul's journey, rather than their physical journey, and that's why this suit was added.

So if you add the cards above (fifty-two) plus the four new princes (fifty-six) plus the twenty-two Major Arcana cards then you will get seventy-eight cards for the now standard tarot deck.

The fifty-six cards are called the Minor Arcana, and the twenty-two spirit cards are called the Major Arcana - minor secrets and major secrets.

The word arcana is the plural of arcanum,
which means profound secret.

The Minor Arcana in the tarot are a collection of basic secrets, and the Major Arcana are a collection of soul secrets. Together the full set of tarot cards explains the secrets within our lives.

Below is a picture of the spirit suit, which is also known as the Major Arcana:

The soul's journey begins

Physical journey on Earth

Mental journey on Earth

Spiritual journey on Earth

You can create your own tarot deck if you purchase a fifty-two card playing deck, add in four prince cards, and then add twenty-two Major Arcana cards. The result is a full set of current tarot cards.

I hope this helps you understand how tarot decks have evolved over the centuries.

Finding a Tarot Deck that Suits You

There are so many tarot decks on the market that it can make you dizzy trying to find one, so don't look yet. Consider your life and what is important to you. Ask yourself questions like;

- Do I prefer being outside more during the day or night? Would I resonate more with pictures of daytime or night-time?
- Do I prefer looking at pictures of elves, forests, or stars, or do I even care about those things?
- Would I like a tarot deck that's specific to a healing modality; e.g., tarot cards with herbs on them?
- Do I want pictures that are close to the original tarot, or am I happy to go with something more creative and artistic?
- Do I want pictures with lots of color or just simple drawings and/or numbers?
- Do I want a tarot deck with writing on the card to remind me what the meaning is?

If you would like a deck that has meanings written on it, then please try my deck: http://www.eleanorhammond.com.au/index.php/store/tarot-cards

There are many tarot decks available and it's worth understanding what you want first before browsing the Internet or stores, as you may be tempted to purchase a deck that doesn't suit you, just because it's on special, or looks pretty.

The difficulty with purchasing a deck online is that you can't hold them in your hands first. The cards may feel too thin or be of poor quality - perhaps printed on cardboard that isn't gloss laminated. Cardboard tarot cards look authentic but age quickly and need replacing regularly. If you're like me, you prefer a long-term relationship with the cards and will be upset if the special cards you purchased show signs of age not long after starting using them.

Tip: Really consider the box that the deck comes in. The soft boxes have a flap on the inside, which makes it hard to push the cards down and can damage the cards over time, and the softer boxes tend to break very quickly. If you have a wooden box and some soft material (most people use silk) to store your new cards in, it doesn't matter what box they come in. If you like to carry your cards around with you, then the box that the cards come in needs to be sturdy to protect them.

Blessing Your Cards

The easiest way of cleansing your cards is to have the intention of clearing old energy off of them as you pick up each card. The power of your intention is all that is really required to ensure your cards stay clean.

Sit quietly and open your deck. Realize that these cards are just a tool for you to use to access your intuitive ability. Obviously it's not the card that assists in any way; it's you accessing your intuition when using the cards. The card is a vehicle for your intuitive ability to unfold, so have gratitude for the tools you use.

Really look at each card and say, "thank you for helping me."

Go through each card in this way. You do not need to know what the cards mean. Just look at the pictures and place the card back in the deck when you feel ready.

Keep your cards wrapped in something that feels beautiful and special to you. Most tarot readers wrap their cards in silk; however, I find that the type of material depends on the climate you live within. Generally, silk will ensure that your cards stand the test of time in most climates.

Putting a crystal like selenite or citrine on top of your deck when you're not using the deck works amazingly well and allows you to cleanse and charge your cards overnight.

I bless my cards by asking for Archangel Michael, or another high vibration and protective energy; dependent on your personal beliefs, to please protect the cards and ensure that any messages coming from the cards are for my highest good.

Creating Safe Space

When you conduct a tarot reading for yourself or others, you cannot access higher guidance if you feel unsafe. We are human, and we have human desires and weaknesses. The biggest one is that we can become closed-minded and only hear what we want to hear when it comes to a reading.

If you, or the person you are reading for, is after a thrill when doing the cards, then you may get one. Likewise, if you say you are open to hearing bad news, then you'll likely get bad news - not necessarily the truth.

If you are after guidance and have a completely open and accepting mind, then you will get guidance. A lot of people want the cards to give them a specific result.

If a person is unhappy in a relationship, then of course they'll want the cards to say that they should leave the relationship and not to try and work things out. If someone really loves a person, then they'll want the cards to show love coming back from the other person. This is the trap that most readers fall into - trying to project what it is that spirit is saying via the cards.

The cards neither love you nor hate you. The cards are a tool for accessing spiritual and higher consciousness guidance.

The steps I use when preparing myself for a reading;

- Clear the room: I conduct readings at the dinner table - the heart of the house to me. I vacuum the room, and clear anything off the table that isn't one of my reading tools - removing clutter that might distract me.
- Create space: I put on a special table cloth, some crystals, a candle, and then play easy listening or meditation music.
- Meditate: The room might be clear, but my mind might be full of clutter. I sit still in silence for at least ten minutes before I do any readings. If any thoughts come up, I simply let them go and sit in silence.
- Raise the vibration: I then say a small prayer to myself. When I conduct readings for other people I say the prayer out loud in front of them so that they can feel assured. The prayer can be anything that makes you feel safe and secure. I always say ***"I ask for higher protective energy to surround me, and higher healing energy to come through me, and I request a reading for my (or the person's) highest good."***

Then I begin.

CHAPTER TWO

The Five Elements and the Five Suits

We are at the beginning now. Please remember: You do not need to remember each word as it's written in this book, as the information will be re-written in different ways to assist in your learning process.

Allow yourself time to relax and enjoy, and I will take you on a learning voyage.

As I wrote already at the beginning of this book - everyone that opens this book will be at various stages with their knowledge of the tarot. This book is designed for anyone as it will give the fundamental teachings to those people who don't know anything about tarot, and it will deepen the knowledge of anyone that does.

The teaching will be the same for every tarot deck.

Water: Our emotions, from sorrow to happiness.

This suit is all about how we feel. We may feel emotionally stable, or unstable. Think about water and how we use water to describe emotions. Someone in a peaceful mood might be considered as calm as a deep pool of water, or an angry person might be considered stormy. We could be in love with a beautiful person one day, and then have turbulent emotions about them the next day. Relationships can make us happy or sad. We can be content with life or feel resolved to make changes.

The water suit might be called chalices, cups, hearts, or anything else that pertains to the water element.

Fire: Our passion and excitement.

Life lessons can be painful and exciting, and occasionally when we are learning our life lessons we metaphorically walk through the fire. We burn ourselves and other people. Passion can be destructive. Passion can give us itchy feet and make us want to travel and experience what life has to offer. Passion pushes the boundaries and lights our internal flame. Without passion we would be bored. A hobby could be a new passion. A person could light our fire. You can have a passionate relationship, or a boring one.

The fire suit might be called wood, clubs, wands, staves, or anything else that pertains to the fire element.

Air: Our thoughts and ability to plan and think ahead.

Do you use your mind to support and help yourself, or do you use your mind to over-think everything and stress yourself? Do you use your thoughts to torture yourself or protect yourself? Do you have clarity of thought? Do you stress other people out? Are you creating a disaster because you haven't thought anything through? Do you always have a lot of ideas floating around in the air?

The air suit might be called knives, swords, spades, smoke, birds, or anything else that pertains to the air element.

Earth: Our ability to feed and clothe ourselves.

People need food, shelter, and clothing to survive. There may be an abundance of food, or extreme poverty and starvation. There is a difference between someone trying to eke out a living close to a fresh-water stream full of fish, and someone trying to live off the land in the desert.

The person that lives near the stream has an abundance of food to eat, and the person living in the desert is surviving on the small amount of food available to them. Anything that comes from the earth – whether it be a home made of stone or wood, or fruit, vegetables and meats to eat, clothing to wear made of cotton or silk or leather, and the ability to purchase items of the earth, is all related to the earth suit.

Generally we do not need to go fishing to get fish now, we get a job, earn money, and use money to buy items of the earth. We do not cut down trees to build a home, or get rocks to build a wall. We work, earn money and pay for these items.

Therefore the earth suit is all about survival and can relate to how well we are doing and how badly we are doing. The earth suit might be called crystals, diamonds, coins, money, pentacles, abundance, or anything else that pertains to the earth element.

Spirit: Our soul's journey and growth.

The Major Arcana, or soul growth, cards were created to describe the enormous perspective shifts which can happen to people without an external event changing life circumstance. For instance, you could stay where you're living, in a bad relationship, with ten kids, no food, and you could become enlightened and blissfully happy. Other people might stop you in the street and ask you what your secret is and how you're always happy under such terrible circumstances. You might say that you had a soul changing experience. You could have everything in life that is considered by others to be horrible and bad, and you could be exceedingly happy.

Conversely, you could have all the things that money can buy, be in a beautiful relationship, have wonderful children, be supported to live the life that you want, and be depressed. It's true that money can't buy happiness. Regardless of your situation in life, you could feel like you haven't learnt anything and that you're going through the same emotional patterns over and over, picking the same type of person for a relationship, with no spiritual progression. Therefore the Major Arcana, or soul growth suit, explains the soul's journey and is the spirit element

The spirit suit might be called pilgrimage, spirit, Major Arcana, soul or anything else that pertains to the spirit element.

Exercises

- If your tarot deck isn't already in order from ace to king or zero to twenty-one, then put them into order.
- Place your tarot deck into five piles with the aces, and The Fool (the zero of the spirit suit) on top. If you are learning with the fifty-two card playing deck, then you will not have a spirit suit and there will only be four piles of cards.
- Put your cups suit in the first pile, then your staves deck in the second pile, then the swords suit, pentacles suit, and if you have it – your spirit suit in the order shown in the picture below.

- Now accessing your intuition with the tarot cards will begin. Repeat this phrase, saying out loud the bold text:
- "**We need love,**" and look at your water suit, **"passion,"** and look at your fire suit, **"mental stimulation,"** and look at your air suit, **"food, shelter, clothing,"** and look at your earth suit, "**and soul growth,**" and look at your spirit suit, **"to survive and prosper"**.
- Take your time and do this process repeatedly until you can go through the entire process without referring back to the phrase in the book.

Discovering the elements

In the below exercise you do not have to remember anything about your cards. Just allow yourself to be comfortable and most importantly, take your time. This exercise may take several days to complete properly, which is fine. If you take the time now, then you will do well later.

- As you look at each cups card, say the word "love" to yourself. Take your time. Pick up each of the cards in the cups suit in turn, repeating the word "love" with each card.
- Look at the way that each cup card was created. What is on the picture for the Ace of Cups card? How is love depicted on this card? What about the Four of Cups card? How about the Seven of Cups card? How is love depicted throughout the suit of cups? It's not always happy or romantic love that is depicted.

The fifty-two card playing deck has the hearts suit. The hearts suit is the water or cups suit.

When we talk about matters of the heart, we generally are talking about emotions. We feel bad, good, in love, have churning emotions, feel disappointed, feel on top of the world or have feelings of long-term love and devotion. Love in all of its forms is shown in the suit of cups.

- As you look at each staves card, say the word "passion" to yourself. Again, take your time. Look through each card within the staves suit, from ace to ten, page, prince, queen, king; repeating "passion" for each card you look at.
- How has each card depicted passion? Is all passion exciting? Or has a passionate occurrence become a battle of endurance?

The fifty-two card playing deck has clubs. The clubs suit is the fire, or staves suit.

It's possible to be passionate about a job, a hobby, a person, a place, or just about anything. We can get more passionate about life, or we can lose our passion for life. Passion is what drives us to be better, and do better. It gives us the internal spark which lights up our eyes when we're excited by life.

- As you look at each swords card, say the phrase "mental stimulation" to yourself. Look through each card within the swords suit, from ace to ten, page, prince, queen, king; repeating the phrase "mental stimulation".

- How has each card depicted 'mental stimulation'? Are some cards showing a lack of mental stimulation with people asleep? Are some cards showing too much mental stimulation with people looking stressed?

The fifty-two card playing deck has the spades suit. The word spade is Italian for the word sword and therefore the spade suit is the air, or swords suit.

We have an ability to think and plan for the future. We also have the ability to worry incessantly about things that we have no control over. What we think about becomes what we plan for (even unconsciously,) and the plans that we make become the lives that we live.

Swords coming up in a reading indicates that calm thought which leads to positive plans is appropriate now. Worrying is not going to help anyone.

- As you look at the pentacles suit, say the phrase "food, shelter and clothing" to yourself.
- Look through each card within the pentacles suit, from ace to ten, page, prince, queen, and king; repeating the phrase "food, shelter and clothing " for each card. What pictures are used to show food, shelter and clothing? Are there cards that show lack and poverty? Are there cards showing abundance?

The fifty-two card playing deck has a diamonds suit. Pentacles are the earth, and diamonds suit.

Each person needs food, shelter, and clothing (and love) to survive and pentacles reflect the earth that provides abundance to us. Nowadays people don't generally go hunting for food or chop down a tree to build shelter. Usually people find a job, get paid, and use the money to buy food, shelter and clothing for themselves.

This is why the earth suit has changed context and become money and career over time.

- As you look at Major Arcana card, say the phrase "soul growth" to yourself.
- Look through each card within this suit, from zero, which is The Fool card to the twenty-second card which is The World card; repeating the words "soul growth" with each card. What pictures did people use to describe a significant soul journey?

All of the Major Arcana cards are soul growth cards.

Spirit walking the earth is reflected within this suit. We are all spirits, with physical human body. The Major Arcana represents the activity of the soul throughout our lives, and does not necessarily reflect the physical journey. There can be times in life where you feel like a massive new beginning is taking place within yourself, which is going to change the course of this lifetime - however people outside of you may not see anything actually happening. An event can change the way we think and feel about a certain place or person. These changes happen in spirit and is usually more life altering than anything that happens outside of us.

The Elements of Life

Now we shall look at the suits from a different perspective. Again, you don't have to remember anything, you just have to follow along. We are not focusing on any one card, we are focusing on the suits: the cups, spades, swords, pentacles and spirit groups.

1. Ask yourself, "What would be the outcome if I started a new job?" or if this questions isn't appropriate for your life circumstances, ask a question similar to this that involves a change in the flow of money into your life.
2. Shuffle your deck and draw three cards.
3. Now look at the three cards that you pulled out;
    *   The WATER (hearts/cups/chalices) suit will show if you will be emotionally attached to your new job. You might love it! If you did draw a water element card, what does the picture look like? Does it feel nice or not?
    *   The FIRE (staves/clubs/wands) suit will show up if you will be passionate about the job. If you did draw a fire element card, what does the picture look like? Does it feel nice or not? You might feel passionately that it would be a mistake to change jobs. The card might show that you will enjoy the physical aspect of the new job, or it might show that the effort and strain physically will be too much for you now.
    *   The AIR (spades/swords/birds/thought) suit will show up if the job will be mentally stimulating. If you did draw an air element card, what does the picture look like? Does it feel nice or not? Will your thoughts be happy, or heavy?
    *   The EARTH (diamonds/pentacles/coins/crystals) suit, if drawn, will reflect how well you will be able to provide for yourself and your family with the new job. If you did draw an earth element card, what does the picture look like? Does it feel nice or not? Does there look like an abundance, or not much at all? Is there richness or poverty?
    *   The SPIRIT (Major Arcana) suit will show up if the job is in line with your soul's highest developmental goals or completely against it! Will the job fulfil your soul growth needs? If you did draw a spirit element card, what does the picture look like? Does it feel nice or not? Does it look like the job would make your soul happy, or sad?

4. Consider the cards that you pulled out. What suit is missing? What two (or more) elements are missing? What does that mean to you? Would the new job be all love, but no money? Would the new job be all passion but no mental stimulation? Would the new job be stressful thinking and no fun?

It's almost impossible to be in complete balance because of a job, or through the work we do. It's hard to find a job that fulfils our money (earth), passion (fire), mental (air), love (water) and soul (spirit) needs. If you have work like that, then you're very lucky and you probably love what you do, and everyone will no doubt love that you're doing it! My job fulfils me in most ways, but I still need my family around me to love, even though I love what I do.

There is a saying - people need three things in order to be happy:

- Someone to love, (water/emotional)
- Something to do, (fire/passion)
- Something to look forward too. (mental ideas and plans)

If we don't have enough food, shelter, or clothing, then we don't care too much about the above three things. So if we have all four things; will we be happy?

No. We also need to feel that we are living within our ideals. Within our soul's purpose. So if we have all five things will we be happy?

Probably.

Look at your piles of cards again;

Look at your cups suit. We need love - the waters of emotion - to fulfil our human needs. We can run a business for money alone, but then we'd probably need to come home to our family, or have a big social life to fulfil our need for love.

Look at your staves suit. We need passion – the fire in our belly - to get anything done. If we have no energy, no passion, no fire for life, then we will just sit back and dream, and dream, and dream. Therefore, if there are no staves (fire) cards in a business idea reading, then the person may be lacking drive and enthusiasm. Sure, the idea might be a good one, but with no energy it will go nowhere.

Look at your swords suit. We need to think ideas through – air time for our thoughts. We need to consider, and sit in quiet contemplation, in order to ensure that we're moving along the path that we want to in life. If we don't think about what we're doing, and were we arc going, then we will drift along in a bit of a mess, or move around and around in circles and never get anything done. Air is about the way we think. We can think clearly, or we can be 'air-heads' and completely confused, with no clear direction or goals.

Too much thinking (air cards) with no action (fire cards) and an idea will never actually get off the ground.

Look at your pentacles suit. We need the earth to provide food, shelter and clothing. These days we get a job, earn money, and then purchase earth's bounty. For instance, we don't need to go fishing to get fish. We get a job, earn money, and buy fish. We don't need to chop down wood to build a house, we get a job, earn money, and buy the house. The earth suit has become the coin suit in a lot of decks now to show the shift away from earth consciousness to money consciousness. We cannot eat our coins, only the food that those coins buy.

Look at your spirit suit. I am not talking about religion when I use the word spirit. I am talking about the being that inhabits your physical form. There is more and more focus on our work needing to fulfil us spiritually. A lot of people will change jobs if their spiritual needs are not being met. More and more people are resigning from positions that they don't feel holds to their own ideals. For instance, a vegan won't work in a sausage factory as it may go against their belief system. They'd do better working on an organic vegetable farm which is more in line with their spirituality, if the vegan eating choice was made due to spiritual reasons rather than simply a food, and physical, choice.

In what order would you put the five elements?

Primitive mankind might have put earth first as they needed to eat, stay warm and keep sheltered to survive. Then perhaps, the air of new ideas so that they could figure out how to grow or catch more food. After this perhaps the fire of passion and energy that kept them moving when they were hungry. Finally the waters of love and emotion to keep communities working together. Spirit has always been important to humankind and there have been many cave paintings depicting higher beings. Spirit may have been placed as the top priority by primitive mankind.

I'm not saying that love isn't important. I'm saying that survival tends to win out over the heart as far as the mass of humankind is concerned.

In what order would you place the elements, and therefore the tarot suits which relate to each element?

- Place the suits in order of priority that makes sense to you in regard to making a decision around getting a new job, and then
- Place the suits in order of priority in regard to your family life.

The above exercise will show you how at different times of our lives, different needs are required to be met.

Do you believe that love (water/cups) is more important than food (earth/pentacles)? Do you believe that passion is more important than mental stimulation? Sure you can have an idea (air/swords), but if you don't have the passion (fire/staves) to do the work, then nothing gets done. So maybe passion (fire) is required in order to come up with ideas (air) that require energy (fire?) This can be considered a circle of sorts.

When we're in survival mode a lot of our passion and ideas comes from trying to feed and clothe ourselves, and stay warm and protected. Emotions are quite a big luxury and we can never have an emotion unless we have a thought first.

"So the mind can rule the emotions?" My student asked me.

"Yes. You have to have a thought 'oh, that was scary,' in order to feel frightened. A thought always comes before an emotion. Even upon waking from a nightmare, you have to have the thought 'oh, that was scary. I was scared,' before the change takes place in the body."

A thought (air/mental) has to happen before an emotion (love/water) happens. Therefore, emotions have to be the most luxurious thing about being a human-being.

Does that make sense to you?

- How would you put it? What phrase would you use yourself in order to describe the sequence of the elements and therefore the suits?

Here is an example of placing the suits in order that pertain to a baby from birth. Would you agree with this?

1. Spirit suit first - a soul has chosen to be here at this time to learn and grow,
2. Earth suit second - a child needs food, shelter and clothing,
3. Fire suit third - a child needs passion in order to scream and cry when it's hungry,
4. Air - a child needs mental stimulation and ideas in order to learn how to speak,
5. Water - a child needs to be loved, and to love, in order to thrive.

You can have the fifty-two card playing deck and do a full reading for someone as it does have most of the elements that sustain us - just not the spirit element.

So let's have a look. In the below five examples I have made up a reading to show how one suit on its own can cause chaos in our lives.

Example One: Jane's business idea - all heart, no brain
If Jane has an idea for a business and the three cards drawn are all water cards, then perhaps Jane has put her heart before her head. Is Jane so in love with the idea of the

business that she hasn't thought sensibly about it? If there's no fire cards she's not going to do anything anyway and, with no air cards, it's likely that Jane hasn't thought the business idea through.

Example Two: Jane's business idea - all passion, no sense

If Jane has an idea for a business and the three cards drawn are all fire cards, then is Jane going to put any thought (air) into her idea? Or is she just all passion and energy but no thought? Jane might be coming out 'guns blazing' only to end up in a heap because she hasn't actually thought anything through.

Example Three: Jane's business idea - all ideas, no energy

If Jane has an idea for a business and the three cards drawn are all air cards, is Jane going to get anything done? Is Jane all talk and good ideas? Having all air cards might be appropriate as Jane might be at the planning/thinking stage of creating the business now. It might not indicate the future, however it might indicate all thought and no action.

If I was to draw all air cards for Jane's business, I might ask her a question like; "Jane, please draw another three cards showing the progress of the business within the next few months."

If Jane then pulls out another three air cards, I'd be counselling her to surround herself with energetic people who like to finish tasks who will motivate Jane to actually progress with the business. If Jane is the sort of person that likes to work alone, then maybe the business idea is not the way for her to go.

Example Four: Jane's business idea - providing for everyone, or being greedy

If Jane has an idea for a business and three cards are drawn and they are all earth cards, perhaps focused more on money than anything else. Has money been the driving force? With no air cards showing, then there may not be enough thought put into the business idea. Within no fire cards showing passion, the business probably won't happen anyway.

Example Five: Jane's business idea - soul journey

If Jane has an idea for a business and the three cards drawn are Major Arcana (spirit) cards, then all bets are off. If Jane chooses to go in the direction of her business idea, then she's in for a major life lesson. Some lessons are wonderful and happy, some however are painful and disappointing. Either way, we are often put into situations where we **have** to learn our lessons before we can move on.

You will now have an understanding why balance is important between the elements. Too much of anything isn't good for us. A fantastic business idea for you will have great ideas (air), give a feeling of passion (fire), bring abundance (earth), happiness (water) and will fulfil a need you have in the world right now (spirit.)

See the word balance in the middle of the star below.

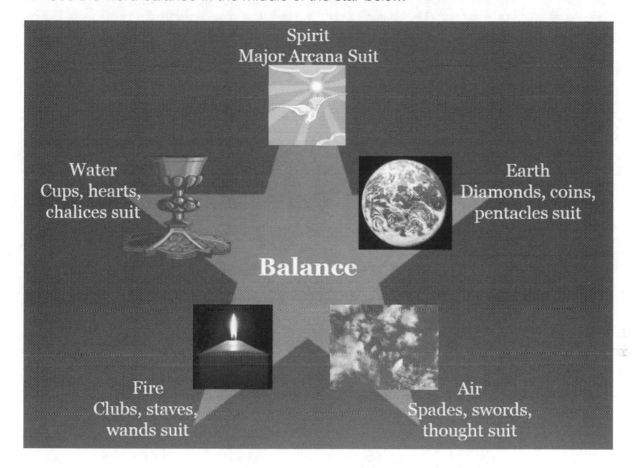

1. Sample Question for Course

Janie wants to know if she'd be happy in a new job and she's drawn a cups/water card. What do you tell her?

    A. No. You are missing too many elements to be happy in the job.

    B. You might be happy. The cups suit is the love and emotions suit, however we will need to check the actual meaning of this specific card to know for sure, as some cups cards can mean an unhappy emotion, or an unrequited love.

    C. Yes, you will be happy in the job.

    D. None of the above apply.

2. Sample Question for Course

Janie wants to know if she'd be happy in a new job and she's drawn an air/swords card. What do you tell her?

    A. No, you are missing too many elements to be happy in the job.

    B. You might be. The swords suit is the thinking and mental stimulation suit however we will need to check the actual meaning of this specific card to know for sure. Some sword cards can mean too little mental stimulation, and other sword cards can mean too much mental stimulation and therefore stress.

    C. Yes, you will be happy in the job.

    D. It's unlikely that you'll be happy, as you're missing the love suit, but you will be mentally stimulated. We will need to check the actual meaning of this specific card to know for sure, as some swords can mean too little mental stimulation (you'd be bored), and other cards can mean too much mental stimulation (you'll be stressed).

3. Sample Question for Course

Which of the below is **most** right. Janie wants to know if she'd be happy in a new job and she's drawn five cards; one from each of the five suits.

    A. Yes. You appear to have all of the elements to enjoy the new job. Let's check the meanings of the individual cards to see how they'll impact you more specifically.

    B. Yes. You appear to have all of the elements required to really enjoy your new job.

    C. Yes. You have a good chance at happiness with this job.

CHAPTER THREE

Minor and Major Arcana cards

As already mentioned, the word arcana is the plural of arcanum which means profound secret. The Minor Arcana in the tarot are a collection of basic secrets and the Major Arcana are a collection of soul secrets. Together the full set of tarot cards explain the secrets within our lives.

The fifty-six Minor Arcana cards represent the physical needs and events that the human body, mind and emotions may go through.

The Major Arcana cards represent the spiritual needs and events and the soul growth journey.

The first four suits (Minor Arcana): water, fire, air, earth is all about our physical needs, desires, emotions, and everything else that is related to being human.

The fifth suit, which is the Major Arcana, is all about our soul and our soul's growth.

Therefore the four suits of the Minor Arcana relate to the physical form. The human body and all the body requires. Physical needs - earth (food), air (mental stimulation), fire (passion), and water (love).

1) Air is our thoughts, beliefs, and energy within our body. Air also describes thoughts and ideas, and Reiki energy. The brain zap-zapping lightning everywhere. Ideas and creativity and plans. Swords cut through the air, and when we speak sharply then we are probably speaking with the mind rather than the heart.

2) Fire is our passion and excitement. It could be what we do for a living but it doesn't have to be what we do for money. Fire is what give us passion. It could be a hobby, it could be a love affair, it could be travel, it could be us having itchy feet and wanting to do things differently – it's the fire within. If we are **all** passion, then we can yell and push people around if we don't have our mind or heart involved in our relationships. Wood burns, and staves/clubs are wood, therefore all wood suits are fire and passion.

3) Water is our emotions. Sometimes we're happy, sad, angry, and heartbroken. We cry tears of joy or of happiness. Our emotions can be stormy or calm, just like the seas. You may have heard phrases such as 'stormy seas' or 'as calm as a deep pool'. These phrases can also be attached to our emotions. Water is emotions, joy, pain, and heart ache. Feeling, rather than thinking. We can hold water in a cup. The cup / heart / chalices suit is the water suit.

4) Earth is all about our practical needs in a physical form, such as food, shelter, and clothing. If we don't have the solid foundation that earth provides, then we don't have the luxury of delving into our passions. We need to eat, sleep in a safe place, and stay warm in winter. Pentacles is all about the physical needs of the body. We usually work for someone else to earn money, and then with that money we purchase the items of the earth that are required for our survival. That's why pentacles are now sometimes called coins or career.

The twenty-two Major Arcana cards are the spiritual happenings, needs and events that the human body, mind and emotions can go through.

5) Spirit is all about our soul growth. The reason why the Major Arcana cards were created was that people could have enormous transformation happen on the inside, and no change might be visible on the outside. For instance, you could stay where you're living, in a bad relationship, with ten kids and no food, but become enlightened and blissfully happy. Other people might stop you in the street and ask you what your secret is and how you're always happy. You might say that you had a soul changing experience.

You could have everything in life that is considered horrible and bad, and you could be exceedingly happy.

Conversely, you could have all the things that money can buy, be in a beautiful relationship, with wonderful children, be supported to live the life that you want, and you could be depressed. It's true that money can't buy you happiness.

Regardless of your situation in life, you could feel like you haven't learnt anything and that you're going through the same emotional patterns repeatedly. You may have repetitive negative thoughts, or work in a boring and dead-end job which you feel trapped in. You may pick the same type of person for a relationship.

Imagine that you were feeling sad one day, and then for no particular reason, and with absolutely no outward event or experience happening, you could have an enormous inward experience of joy which changes your whole outlook on life. That's why the soul cards were developed, because they explain more about where people are with their soul growth journey. It also explains what their spiritual challenges are.

CHAPTER FOUR

The Beginning of Each Journey

"It's a lot easier to say when something ended rather than when it began. Most of us can recognize the end from a mile away, but the beginning always slips up on us, lulling us into thinking what we're living through is yet another moment, in yet another day."

Steve Yarbrough

The Aces and The Fool

A baby must have all of the elements to survive. If a baby has only love (the water element), then it will starve. Without the four elements, spirit (the fifth element,) will release its hold on the human body and return home. All elements must be present in order for a human being to be born and grow in a healthy way.

Let's consider the aces of the suits and the zero of the spirit suit. The new beginning cards for each of the elements.

- The Ace of Cups is a new beginning of a love (water) journey.
- The Ace of Staves is a new beginning of a passionate (fire) journey.
- The Ace of Swords is a new beginning of a mentally stimulating (air) journey.
- The Ace of Pentacles is the new beginning of a journey which will bring abundance (earth) - food, shelter and clothing.
- The Fool is a new beginning of a soul growth (spirit) journey.

Ace of Cups: New Love

Look at your ace of water/cups/heart card. You give love to a baby so that it will feel loved and prosper. New love can indicate a new partner, or a refreshing new beginning within a current relationship. New love can mean that your heart is opening again to a person that you're already in a relationship with. The Ace of Cups can indicate unconditional love in all of its glory. The ace is a one. If one person is in love, and the other person doesn't feel love, the love indicated can be destructive. New or unlimited love is shown by the Ace of Cups. Love and joy are flowing peacefully into and out from your heart.

The Ace of Cups is the card of unconditional and all-encompassing love and you may feel like your heart is overflowing with joy. This card may imply that new love may be coming in the form of a baby, a partner, a pet, or a wonderful new friend. It can also mean that current relationships are receiving a boost and love is blossoming anew. When this card appears in the advice space in a reading, everyone needs to open their hearts - even if they don't want too.

Ace of Staves: New Passion

Look at your ace of fire/staves/wands/clubs. You keep a baby warm and be passionate about caring for it to keep it alive and healthy. Passion comes from the fire suit and is therefore connected to heat and energy. Remember, it's friction that creates heat, so only things that are actually moving can be hot. This is the suit of **doing**, and achieving! The Ace of Staves implies passion – never ending, ever flowing, and it reflects all kinds of passion coming in. Passion is what gets us out of bed in the morning and passion and fire and energy is what gets us through each day. Passion may reflect your passion around a traditional career, and can also reflect a new hobby that has you excited.

The ace is those things that are new and exciting or those things that give people new rushes of energy. New business ideas, new hobbies, taking a physical risk - e.g. bungee jumping, or simply starting to exercise, are all indicated by this card. This ace can indicate that a new hobby is required to give you back a spark of passion if you've been feeling drained and bored by life. Energy is on the increase with this card. New ideas which make you feel powerful and energized are around. If this card is in the advice space in a reading, then it's a strong indication that new energy is required now. If this card is placed in the advice position then you're being asked by spirit to become more passionate about life and start something new.

Ace of Swords: New Idea

Look at your ace of air/swords/spades card. You have to be thoughtful, and use your mind to consider the needs of the baby to ensure its survival and growth. Air is all about the thought processes, new thoughts, new ideas and using the mind as a tool to progress your life and the lives of the people around you. The Ace of Swords reflects what we think and the energy flow within our bodies. The never ending, ever flowing, lightning bolt of new ideas and energy.

This card can show up if people need to be in a career working as an energy worker, e.g. Reiki. This card reflects new ideas, or new plans for your life, and new energy for you because of these plans. As swords are thought and energy, generally they mean **planning** rather than **doing**. This card indicates that people are gaining clarity of thought. Confusion is clearing up for everyone involved. If in the advice position, the Ace of Swords reflects that people need to clear their minds of unnecessary thoughts and only think positive thoughts that improve their life, and the lives of those around them.

Ace of Pentacles: New Abundance

Look at your ace of earth/pentacles/diamonds/coins card. You need to feed, shelter and clothe your baby to keep it healthy and growing. Physical sustenance comes from the earth, however these days we get a job and get money and buy everything we need which is why this suit is sometimes called coins or career. The Ace of Pentacles implies abundance - the never ending, ever flowing, and perhaps new intake of all kinds of abundance.

Abundance is food, shelter, and clothing. All of those things that are needed to sustain the human body. People go shopping to buy food rather than go hunting and gathering generally. Therefore this card now can represent new money coming in and possibly a new career, or even that emotionally all will be well and all your physical needs will be met. If this card is in the advice position in a reading, then there is a need to open up to a new beginning of some kind – a new job, home, or maybe even a change of career, or another kind of new beginning.

0 - The Fool: the soul's journey begins

Look at The Fool card. There are many differing beliefs around what a soul or a spirit actually is. For the purposes of this course, and in learning the tarot, the soul is that life spark which is connected to a larger, or higher, consciousness – a God consciousness, in whatever form your idea of God takes for you. If that magical spark of life doesn't come into a human body, then a human life stays limp and lifeless. Therefore The Fool card in the spirit suit can indicate a new or healthy baby, or a whole new journey within your current life. A complete new beginning is indicated for you.

The picture I have drawn for The Fool is meant to resemble the light of the soul inside a fetus. Literally a baby and a soul joining together. We are often The Fool at the beginning of anything we do. We lack knowledge and grace. We take risks and start fresh.

The Fool, as it's known in the traditional tarot is the beginning of the soul's journey. As a baby is considered the beginning of the soul's journey here on earth, occasionally this card can indicate an actual baby. More likely though, this card is indicating a major new change for the person being read for. If this card has shown up around a new career, falling in love, or starting a new business idea, then the message is always look before you leap!

Note that both The Fool and the Ace of Cups can indicate a baby, as can some other cards. One is a new beginning - the soul's journey starting fresh, and the other is a new relationship or an overflowing feeling of heart connection.

Examples of what this card may mean when it comes up in a reading are below:

- Falling in love; lover's leap. That frightening leap into the unknown with a new love interest.
- A new job.
- A pregnancy and a new soul coming to earth.
- The start of a major new lifecycle in the life of the person being read for.
- Lack of preparation or forethought before embarking on a major change.

There are many new births and new growths in a lifetime. We give birth to new business ideas, create new art, fall in love with a new partner, start to learn something for the first time.

Anytime that we do something new we are embarking on a new adventure, we are having a new beginning and it's a birth of something new.

Consider this; The Fool asks us to take a leap of faith or. This may be risky. The Fool is also a warning indicating a new to beware – we may be taking too much of a risk right now.

You could have something physical happen where there is NO RISK; you could start a new job which would be the Ace of Pentacles, as well as a new relationship which would be the Ace of Cups, as well as a new hobby which would be the Ace of Staves, as well as a whole new idea which would be the Ace of Swords.

If however you had a new job that was very risky, then you might draw The Fool with the Ace of Pentacles.

If you have fallen head over heels and crazy in love, then you could draw The Fool with the Ace of Cups.

If you have a new idea which is something so different for you and a big risk for you to take, then you might draw The Fool with the Ace of Swords.

Exercise: The Ace of Cups

Look at your Ace of Water/Cups/Heart card again and this time think of your own life. If you were creating a tarot deck, would you call this suit the cups or water suit, or would you call it something else entirely?

What would you call it? _____

Write down ten examples where you have had the Ace of Cups energy in your life. Don't focus on trying to be right, just go with what **feels** right for you. Go back to the previous chapter and re-read that if you need too.

1) Example: the day I met my husband. The day my baby was born. When I decided to start again in my current relationship, and open my heart back up to him.

_____

2)

_____

3)

_____

4)

_____

5)

_____

6)

_____

7)

_____

8)

_____

9)

_____

10)

_____

Draw your idea of what this card looks like to you.

Exercise: The Ace of Staves

Look at your Ace of Fire/Staves/Wands/Clubs and this time think of your own life. If you were creating a tarot deck, would you call this suit the staves, fire or energy suit, or would you call it something else entirely?

What would you call it? _____

Write down ten examples where you have had the Ace of Staves energy in your life. Don't focus on trying to be right, just go with what **feels** right for you. Go back to the previous chapter and re-read that if you need too.

1) Example: when I first started dance class, or when I first started my business.

_____

2)

_____

3)

_____

4)

_____

5)

_____

6)

_____

7)

_____

8)

_____

9)

_____

10)

_____

Draw your idea of what this card looks like to you.

Exercise: The Ace of Swords

Look at your Ace of Air/Swords/Spades card and this time think of your own life. If you were creating a tarot deck, would you call this suit the swords or air suit, or would you call it something else entirely?

What would you call it? _____

Write down ten examples where you have had the Ace of Swords energy in your life. Don't focus on trying to be right, just go with what feels right for you. Go back to the previous chapter and re-read that if you need too.

1) Example: when I first had a new business idea. When I suddenly changed the way I thought about everything. When he/she knifed me in the back? Remember, tarot describes all of life. Often readers will just give the more positive view.

_____

2)

_____

3)

_____

4)

_____

5)

_____

6)

_____

7)

_____

8)

_____

9)

_____

10)

_____

Draw your idea of what this card looks like to you.

Exercise: The Ace of Pentacles

Look at your Ace of Earth/Pentacles/Diamonds/Coins card and think of your own life. If you were creating a tarot deck, would you call this suit the pentacles, earth or coins suit, or would you call it something else entirely?

What would you call it? _____

Write down ten examples where you have had the Ace of Pentacles energy in your life. Don't focus on trying to be right, just go with what feels right for you. Go back to the previous chapter and re-read that if you need too.

1) Example: when I started the new job. When I won some money. When a baby came into the family. When I went shopping for food earlier today.

_____

2)

_____

3)

_____

4)

_____

5)

_____

6)

_____

7)

_____

8)

_____

9)

_____

10)

_____

Draw your idea of what this card looks like to you.

Exercise: The Fool

The soul's journey begins. Look at The Fool card and think of your own life. If you created a tarot deck, would you call this suit the Major Arcana or spirit suit, or something else entirely?

What would you call it? _____

Write down ten examples where you have had The Fool energy in your life. Don't focus on trying to be right, just go with what **feels** right for you. Go back to the previous chapter and re-read that if you need too.

1) e.g., when I took a risk on that person coming into my life. When I tripped over my own feet yesterday. When I jumped into that job without checking the details. When I travelled overseas.

_____

2)

_____

3)

_____

4)

_____

5)

_____

6)

_____

7)

_____

8)

_____

9)

_____

10)

_____

Draw your idea of what this card looks like to you.

4. Sample Question for Course

Janie wants to fall pregnant and when you ask her to draw a card in relation to her chances, you get the Ace of Swords. What do you tell her?

A. It's unlikely that you'll fall pregnant right now.
B. The ace is new beginnings, so that's good, but the swords indicates that you may need to think about your situation from a different angle. Maybe try Reiki or some other alternative idea to assist you in falling pregnant.
C. Yes, new beginnings is indicated by the ace, so it looks like you'll definitely have a baby.

5. Sample Question for Course

Janie wants to fall pregnant and when you ask her to draw a card in relation to her chances, she pulls out the Ace of Cups. What do you tell her?

A. It's unlikely that you'll fall pregnant right now.
B. The ace is new beginnings, so that's good, and the cups indicates love. There is definitely new love around you, so there's a very good chance that this means you will fall pregnant.
C. The ace is new beginnings, so that's good. You may fall pregnant, but you and your partner may be needing to take a trip somewhere different and romantic in order to help the process along.

6. Sample Question for Course

Janie wants to start a new business and when you ask her to draw three cards, she pulls out all cups and swords. What do you tell her?

A. We have love and mental stimulation around your business which is a great thing, but there are no money cards, so it probably won't make you any money.
B. We have love and mental stimulation around your business which is a great thing, you should really go ahead with it and will regret it if you don't.
C. We have love and mental stimulation around your business which is a great thing, but are you passionate about it? With all the air cards, it looks like you put a lot of thought into it, but don't have the passion to actually make it work.
D. We have love and mental stimulation around your business which is a great thing but, do you have the energy for the business right now? Are you sure it's going to bring you the money you'll need?

CHAPTER FIVE

The Second Step: Further Categorizations of the Cards

Who can help you/me?

Now you may have expected me to jump straight in and talk about the two cards within the deck, as I went into so much detail immediately around the aces and The Fool. The ace of a suit is obviously the number one (1) of that suit; as it's the beginning card of each suit. You wouldn't start counting a deck of cards from number three, you'd always start at one. One's therefore always mean the beginning of a journey, or something new. Either physical, mental or emotional.

Rather than go in-depth now around the twos, it's appropriate to discuss the other groupings within the tarot.

This section is focused on how abundance comes into our lives. Consider this, if you wanted something e.g., a loaf of bread, you could:

1. ***Get it yourself.*** You could make a loaf of bread, or go to the store, or ask someone to get it for you. Other people still might help you, and spirit is always working with you, but the main effort right now for the next steps has to come from you. You have to ask someone or do something, in order for you to get a loaf of bread.
2. ***Someone could get it for you.*** They could cook the loaf of bread for you, or they could go to the shop and purchase it for you.
3. ***Spirit could drop it in your lap!*** Spirit might organize for some complete stranger to come by and hand you one unexpectedly.

The third way does happen. Have you ever thought about someone, and then the next day you have bumped into them at the shop? This is spirit's way of bringing people to you. Remember this when you do readings for yourself. Sometimes people can't understand how things can happen, because they're unaware that they're yet to meet a person who's significant in helping them, or they're yet to walk out of the shop and bump into someone that's required in their lives right now.

It's more likely that there are events still unfolding that spirit is trying to work out for you. Spirit might be trying to put a newspaper into your hands so that you see a job being advertised, or you might coincidentally meet someone who can help you find work. You still need to help yourself in order for anything to happen in your life, but spirit might be trying very hard to help you if a Spirit card has shown up.

There is a word that I have created which I use all of the time in my readings for other people. It's ***in-spirit-oration.*** We often say that inspiration comes from left field meaning that all of a sudden we are struck by an amazing idea or thought. To me, spirit gives us the information when we are ready for it, and therefore inspiration is actually in-***spirit***-oration. Spirits are actually talking to us, handing us wonderful ideas. Helping us decide on spur the moment decisions, and plan for longer term goals.

The other word that I like to play with is the word coincidence. Many people are amazed every day when things happen coincidentally. Can I say that ***everything*** is a coincidence if you change the meaning of the word? There is a mathematical term around the word co-incidence. It means that everything happens in perfect alignment. I believe that our lives are filled with instances of co-incidence, where spirit can bring us coincidental events.

So all coincidence is, is spirit making things happen in ***perfect co-incidence***.

Therefore you can see now that when I say that spirit helps us, it could be by providing inspiration, or it could be by a strange series of coincidences. Very rarely does 'spirit help' mean that someone comes knocking on your door wearing white, winged and providing us with the answers to all of life's mysteries. It has been known to happen though. ☺

I believe that spirit does more for us than we'd ever realize, and mostly spirit works through us in the form of our connection to our higher selves (God, or whatever you wish to call this higher power that we are all connected too.) Spirit can actually organize for a person to come into our lives. Therefore spirit might work with someone else, or they might work with us.

So now we can place the tarot cards into another three different groupings:

- Numbers cards: The Ace (one), two, three, four, five, six, seven, eight, nine and ten. Giving us a total of forty cards.
- Court cards: Page, prince, queen and king, giving us a total of sixteen cards.
- Spirit cards: The Fool, through to The World, giving us a total of twenty-two cards.
- When we again look at the way people and things come into our life, it's more likely that we have to do most things ourselves. Therefore the group with the most number of cards in it is related to us doing things for ourselves.
- Doing everything for ourselves is depicted when we draw a card from the <u>numbers</u> group.
- Other people doing things for us is depicted when we draw a card from the <u>court cards</u> group.
- Spirit helping us line up important events in our lives is depicted when we draw a card from the <u>spirit cards</u> suit. This indicates a need to flow with your life and allow spirit to assist you.

Exercise One: Who can help you/me?

Remember: You don't know everything about the individual cards that you have in your hands yet. Don't take any answers you get seriously at this stage, as the meaning of the actual card can change the answer significantly. This exercise is just a way of getting you to understand the three different ways that we get things.

Try this very simple exercise:

- Shuffle your deck.
- Ask a question about how something can come into your life. For instance, you might ask "I need help right now, who can help me?"
- Draw one card.

If the tarot card is a Numbers card, then this means you will have to go out and get the job for yourself. You are the one that has to put the effort in.

If the tarot card is a Court card, then another person will help you get a job. It still means you might have to put the effort in, but the job will come to you via some other person that you need to connect with.

If the tarot card is a Spirit card then spirit is going to drop the job right into your lap (maybe.) You need to follow any inspiration you get, e.g., "I feel I have to go and talk to Mrs. French about a job" etc.

Try this again a few times. Think of another couple of questions that you can ask, and then draw only one card.

Then see if you get a numbers card, a court card, or a spirit card.

7. Sample Question for Course

Janie wants to know what she has to do in order to get a job, you ask the question for her and draw one card. The card is a numbers card, what do you tell her?

- A. Spirit is helping you, don't worry.
- B. You are yet to meet someone that can help you.
- C. There is still things you have to do to help yourself.

8. Sample Question for Course

Janie wants to know what she has to do in order to get a job, you ask the question for her and draw one card. The card is a Court card, what do you tell her?

- A. Spirit is helping you, don't worry.
- B. You are yet to meet someone that can help you, but you still have to be active in pursuing a job.
- C. There is still things you have to do to help yourself.

9. Sample Question for Course

Janie wants to know what she has to do in order to get a job, you ask the question for her and draw one card. The card is a Spirit card, what do you tell her?

A. Spirit is helping you, don't worry, but please remain active in looking for work.
B. You are yet to meet someone that can help you.
C. There is still things you have to do to help yourself.

10. Sample Question for Course

Asking what she has to do in order to get a job, Janie pulls out a Spirit card. Does that mean that she can relax and wait for things to happen?

A. Yes, Janie needs to trust spirit to bring everything to her that she needs to get a job. Her main challenge is learning how to trust the process of life.
B. No. Janie needs to trust that spirit is helping her, but still has to get out and help herself.

CHAPTER SIX

Working out Time Frames

The spirit world is timeless, not functioning in linear time. As far as spirit is concerned, we live forever. However we here on the planet often want to know when something is going to happen and spirit often ignores us when we ask.

There are time frames in the tarot, however they come with a big warning. We all have free will, which means that the more people involved in something, the higher the risk of someone changing their mind. Which can impact the overall outcome as well as the timing.

Consider this: Three friends want to go on an overseas holiday together. One of the friends go to a tarot reader and asks "when will we go overseas together?" and she gets the answer next year. This will be absolutely correct at this moment in time. However tomorrow, one of the friends could say "I've changed my mind. I don't want to go, and I have to save up for a car." This has therefore changed the shared future. If the first friend goes back to a tarot reader and asks "when will all three of us go overseas together?" Then the answer might be never, and both readings could be one day apart.

Do you see the issue with asking for time frames?

Often people tell me "Eleanor, your timings are so spot on!" I think that's because I explain the dangers of time frames so that when things don't work to the time seen in a reading, then people are aware of what could have happened.

I always make sure that I tell people "there is no time on the other side. When we ask questions about time frames, we often don't get an accurate answer, as too many people can change your current future. We can certainly ask though."

There is an easy way to remember which suits correspond best to which time frames.

Cups: Water flows quickly. It doesn't take long to drink a cup of water. Cups denotes days. Emotions can change quickly, and often more frequently than from day to day. If you ask for a time frame and draw out the Six of Cups, then the time frame is six days.

Wands: Fire burns quickly. You can put out a raging fire with some water pretty quickly. You can **burn** through time so quickly. "Wands is weeks" is a nice way of saying it, remembering that fire, wands, and staves are all the fire suit. Wood can burn and they are all wood. Fire can burn through a forest very quickly or very slowly depending on what happens with rainfall and the wind. Therefore if you ask a time frame question and receive the Seven of Staves, then the answer is seven weeks.

Swords: Planning takes time. Swords denotes months. "Swords cut through air" is the phrase I use to remember that the sword is the air element. Air is thought and when thought is put into action, these become plans. It generally takes time to plan properly. Therefore if you ask a time frame question and receive the Two of Swords, then the answer is two months.

Pentacles: Earth rotates once a year. The Earth rotates on its axis once every year, and the pentacles suit denotes the Earth. The Earth rotates around the sun once every year, therefore when asking about a time frame, the pentacles reflect how many times the Earth has rotated and therefore how many years are to pass. If you ask a timeframe question and receive the Two of Pentacles, then you are being told two years.

Spirit: If a Spirit card is drawn from the deck, then you are being told that spirit is trying to organize events for you in order to either bring what you want closer in time, or remove it from your time-line altogether. Sometimes what we want to have happen isn't for our highest good, and spirit will send us on a different path.

NB: A lot of people who read tarot will give a more overall answer to a question. Rather than saying the "two of pentacles is two years" they will say "it's going to happen in two. Two days, or two weeks, or two months, or two years." The reason why this happens is there's differences of opinion on how to use the tarot to depict timeframes. I'm comfortable and happy to use cups as days, staves as weeks, swords as months, pentacles as years, however you may feel comfortable with a different process – and as long as you are clear on what that is before you draw a card, then the timeframe will be accurate.

Now we need to talk about the numbering of the cards and how you can use your tarot cards to find out more information around time frames. Again, we will go over these and you will have time to learn them, so just read through for now and don't try to remember everything. In this section we are focusing mainly on the Minor Arcana. The fifty-six cards are the fourteen cards which make up each of the four suits.

- Your water (chalices, cups, and hearts) suit has fourteen cards in it.
- Your fire (wood, clubs, wands, and staves) suit has fourteen cards in it.
- Your air (knives, swords, spades, smoke and birds) suit has fourteen cards in it.
- Your earth (crystals, diamonds, coins, money, pentacles, and abundance) suit has fourteen cards in it.
- Your spirit (Major Arcana and soul) suit has twenty-two cards in it. Though occasionally an author will add an extra card as the wild card.

We mentioned already that:

- Your water suit is days.
- Your fire suit is weeks.
- Your air suit is months.
- Your earth suit is years.

Therefore, we could put the four suits into the following order:

Cups first as water can flow from a cup very quickly, and the human body would die quickly without water. The King of Cups denotes fourteen days.

Staves second as fire moves quickly, however water can put out fire, and it can take a while for a fire to light. Humans still require heat, however can wear a jumper rather than light a fire. The King of Staves denotes fourteen weeks.

Sword third, as wind can impact both fire and water, and is generally felt the most when it's raining or there's a fire. The King of Swords denotes fourteen months.

Pentacles fourth, as the earth rotates once every year. The King of Pentacles is a long time to wait - fourteen years!

Review the table below:

Cups = Days	Staves = Weeks
Ace = one day	Ace = one week
Two = two days	Two = two weeks
Three = three days	Three = three weeks
Four = four days	Four = four weeks
Five = five days	Five = five weeks
Six = six days	Six = six weeks
Seven = seven days	Seven = seven weeks
Eight = eight days	Eight = eight weeks
Nine = nine days	Nine = nine weeks
Ten = ten days	Ten = ten weeks
Page = eleven days	Page = eleven weeks
Knight = twelve days	Knight = twelve weeks
Queen = thirteen days	Queen = thirteen weeks
King = fourteen days	King = fourteen weeks
Swords = Months	**Pentacles = Years**
Ace = one month	Ace = one year
Two = two months	Two = two years
Three = three months	Three = three years
Four = four months	Four = four years
Five = five months	Five = five years
Six = six months	Six = six years
Seven = seven months	Seven = seven years
Eight = eight months	Eight = eight years
Nine = nine months	Nine = nine years
Ten = ten months	Ten = ten years
Page = eleven months	Page = eleven years
Knight – twelve months	Knight = twelve years
Queen = thirteen months	Queen = thirteen years
King = fourteen months	King = fourteen years

Now consider that there are fifty-two weeks in a year. If you wanted too, you could ask what week in the year will I see someone? Then draw one card, and check the week number from the above table.

For instance, if I wanted to know when I would meet up with a person again next year and I asked that question and drew out the Queen of Swords, I would assume that I will see that person in thirteen months from now, or within the forty-first week of the year.

This is one of the reasons why the question we ask before drawing out a card is so important. A better question to ask is "which **week** within the year will I see that person again?" Then drawing out the Queen of Swords would definitely reflect the forty-first week of the year, rather than thirteen months from now.

Whatever the list is, if it has an obvious first then it can be adapted to your tarot deck. For instance, when reciting the calendar, you always start with January.

Look briefly at the table below, remember again that you do not need to remember this now. This knowledge will be gained throughout the book so just relax and move with me at your own time.

Month	Card
January	Ace of any suit
February	Two of any suit
March	Three of any suit
April	Four of any suit
May	Five of any suit
June	Six of any suit
July	Seven of any suit
August	Eight of any suit
September	Nine of any suit
October	Ten of any suit
November	Page of any suit
December	Knight of any suit
I'm not meant to know	Queen of any suit
I'm not meant to know	King of any suit

When I do readings, I wait until time frames repeat before I mention them.

As an example, if someone asks for a time frame around when something might happen and the current date is the first of June, I ask for one card for the actual month, and if they give me a six, then that might mean June, the month we are in. So then I might ask another question "what season" and if they give me an air card then that's winter (as I mentioned previously I'm in the Southern Hemisphere and it's winter during June here.) So again, I have another card potentially meaning this month. Then I might ask a more direct question, how long until this actually happens, and they give me the Six of Cups, which is six days. Then we have the same timeframe three times!

All three cards are agreeing that the time frame for the event is this month, and probably within six days.

If I wanted too, I could ask for another card to see "what week within the year this will happen". If I got the Ten of Staves which is the twenty-sixth week, then I could add up the weeks in the calendar and be amazed that again, we have the middle of June. I have to say, there is a use for using the cards to find the weeks within the year but I don't usually use this as a tool for time frames as it can take too long to work out when I'm in the middle of a reading.

As you can see from the above example, the way that we phrase a question is critical to ensuring a successful reading.

Exercise: When will it happen?

Try this very simple exercise:

1. Shuffle your deck.
2. Ask a question about when something can come into your life. For instance, you might ask "when will we fall pregnant?"
3. Draw one card.
    *   If the tarot card is a cup, then look on the card at how many days. For instance, if you have pulled out the Seven of Cups, then the answer is seven days.
    *   If the tarot card is a stave, then look on the card at how many weeks. For instance, if you have pulled out the Ace of Staves, then the answer is one week.
    *   If the tarot card is a sword, then look on the card at how many months. For instance, if you have pulled out the Three of Swords, then the answer is three months.
    *   If the tarot card is a pentacle, then look on the card at how many years. For instance, if you have pulled out the Nine of Pentacles, then the answer is nine years.
    *   If the tarot card is a spirit card, then you're usually not meant to know. Have a look at the card and see if you can see something which equates to a cup, stave, sword or pentacle to you. If nothing jumps out at you then it's likely that the answer is you're not meant to know. Please don't jump ahead in this book and see what that particular card means. We are doing this exercise just to look at the different time frame categories inside the tarot deck.
    *   Try this again a few times. Think of another couple of questions that you can ask, and then draw only one card.

Seasons: Time Frame

Another way of splitting up the tarot cards is by season. You really need to be aware of the seasons that are appropriate to where you live. For instance, I live in Australia, and grew up in a town where it rained all through summer, and was dry during winter. Therefore to me the:

- Water suit is the **summer** suit as it usually rains to the point of flooding.
- Fire suit is **autumn**, where all the leaves turn golden and the sun is starting to fade, where we sit in the sunshine and draw in the warmth.
- Air suit is **winter**. The cold winds cutting through our coats making us shiver and huddle inside. That time of introspection and withdrawal.
- Earth suit is **spring**. Earth's bounty coming to harvest when all the fruit and vegetables grow luxuriously.

Now you might consider that the fire suit best denotes summer. The sun is burning its brightest. That is true and fine. As long as you are clear in your own mind about how the cards classify into each season, then do it the way that feels right to you. You do not have to agree with me, or do it my way. This course is about finding your own inner guide and learning from ***inner-tuition***.

Exercise: When Will it Happen

Try this timeframe exercise again, however this time we are going to add in the season:

1. Shuffle your deck.
2. Ask a question about when something can come into your life. For instance, you might ask "what season will we fall pregnant?" Remember that the exact words you use when asking a question is paramount to getting the right answer.
3. Draw one card.
   - If the tarot card is a cups, then the answer is you'll likely fall pregnant in summer.
   - If the tarot card is a stave, then the answer is you'll likely fall pregnant in autumn.
   - If the tarot card is a swords, then the answer is you'll likely fall pregnant in winter.
   - If the tarot card is a pentacles, then the answer is you'll likely fall pregnant in spring.
   - If the tarot card is a spirit card, then have a look at the card and see if you can see something which equates to a season for you. Does it feel cool like winter? Does it feel warm or sunny like autumn or summer? When you draw out a spirit card, you are being asked to look more closely for guidance. Please don't read ahead to find out the meaning of a particular spirit card at this time. If you cannot find a meaning within the card by looking at it, then the answer is you're not meant to know.

Try this again a few times. Think of another couple of questions that you can ask, and then draw only one card.

11. Sample Question for Course
Janie has asked for a time frame around getting a job, what do you tell her?

    A. Time frames are difficult to get right as many different people are involved in the process of filling a vacancy. The people involved have free will, which can impact the timeframes involved. For instance, the person that interviews you might decide tomorrow to have two weeks holidays. We can still draw one card and have a look at the timeframe, however be aware that the timeframe may change.

    B. Spirit is organizing the job for you. Be patient and relax and wait but, we can still draw one card and have a look at the expected time frame for today.

    C. There is no point asking for time frames as too many people can make too many changes in life.

12. Sample Question for Course
Janie has asked for a time frame around getting a job, and has pulled out one card which is the Two of Pentacles, what do you tell her?

    A. The cards are saying it could be two years before you get a job.

    B. Spirit doesn't like to give out time frames, so this may not be a time frame. This card means two years however, it's likely that it means something else is required in order for you to get a job, and that you shouldn't be asking questions about time frames until you've done all the work that you need to around getting a job. Sit back and relax now, as spirit is taking care of everything for you.

    C. Spirit doesn't like to give out time frames, so this may not be a time frame. This card means two years, however it's likely that it means something else is required in order for you to get a job, and that you shouldn't be asking questions about time frames until you've done all the work that you need to around getting a job. Your job right now is to organize yourself and get out there and find a job. Maybe draw another card and we will do ask who can help you with finding a job.

13. Sample Question for Course
Which of the below answers is the most right.
Janie has asked if time frames given by tarot cards are accurate.

    A. There is no time on the other side, and when we ask questions about time frames, we often don't get accurate answers when too many people can change your current future.

    B. Spirit doesn't like to give out time frames, so any time frame might be wrong or right depending on the question you ask.

    C. Spirit doesn't like to give out time frames. Often the cards we draw are an indication of time, however things have to happen in order for a correct time frame to be pulled out of the deck.

14. Sample Question for Course

Janie has asked a time frame question and pulled out the Five of Staves. What time frame is this?

    A. Five weeks.
    B. Five days.
    C. Five years.
    D. Five months.

15. Sample Question for Course

Janie has asked a time frame question and pulled out the Ace of Pentacles. What time frame is this?

    A. One year.
    B. 12 months.
    C. Anytime within the next year.
    D. All of the above.

16. Sample Question for Course

Janie has asked a time frame question and pulled out The Chariot Major Arcana card. What time frame is this?

    A. One year.
    B. Seven months.
    C. Anytime within the next few years.
    D. There is no time frame available to Janie right now.

17. Sample Question for Course

Janie has asked how many weeks until she sees her family again and pulls out a spirit card. Which is the answer to give to Janie?

    A. One year.
    B. Seven months.
    C. Anytime within the next few years.
    D. There is no time frame available to Janie right now. It doesn't mean that it's never going to happen. It means that there are many people involved who need to make the decision for a timeframe to become obvious.

The Alphabet

Now look at how tarot can show the alphabet:

Suit	Letter
Ace of any suit	A, B
Two of any suit	C, D
Three of any suit	E, F
Four of any suit	G, H
Five of any suit	I, J
Six of any suit	K, L
Seven of any suit	M, N
Eight of any suit	O, P
Nine of any suit	Q, R
Ten of any suit	S, T
Page of any suit	U, V
Prince of any suit	W, X
Queen of any suit	Y, Z
King of any suit	I'm not meant to know the letter

During a reading people often wish to know who it is that is indicated by certain events. For instance, it's very handy to have foreknowledge of the initials of a new love interest who is depicted within the reading.

18. Sample Question for Course

Jenny has asked for the name of the person who she is to meet this year and you draw three cards on her behalf and draw out two aces and a king. What do you tell her?

A. Someone whose initials start with an A or B is indicated, however that may not be accurate as the king means that you're not meant to know yet. Aces are all new beginnings though, so I can tell you that the person is new to you.
B. Someone whose initials start with an A or B is indicated.
C. Someone with the initials A or B is indicated however it may be a name that you don't recognize on meeting them. For instance you might meet a person called Mark and not realize until later that their second name is Anthony.

Star Signs

One of the easiest way to identify someone is by their birthday, and birth months are easy to spot in a reading. Two consecutive cards in the same suit indicate a star sign or important month. It has to be the same suit for this to work.

If you have drawn out cards and have:

- The Ace and Two of Cups in the same reading. This indicates an Aquarian or January/February birthday.
- The Ace of Cups and Two of Staves in the same reading. This means nothing as the cards are not in the same suit.
- The Seven and Eight of Swords in the same reading. This indicates a Leo star sign, or a July/August birth month as the numbers are consecutive and in the same suit.
- The Seven of Swords and the Eight of Cups in the same reading. This does not show a star sign as both cards are not in the same suit.
- The Nine and Ten of Swords in the same reading. This indicates a Libra star sign or September/October birthday.
- As long as it is the same suit that shows up, you can work out the birth month. Have a look at the below table:

Card	Star Sign
Ace of any suit with the two of the same suit	Aquarian
Two of any suit with the three of the same suit	Pisces
Three of any suit with the four of the same suit	Aries
Four of any suit with the five of the same suit	Taurus
Five of any suit with the six of the same suit	Gemini
Six of any suit with the seven of the same suit	Cancer
Seven of any suit with the eight of the same suit	Leo
Eight of any suit with the nine of the same suit	Virgo
Nine of any suit with the ten of the same suit	Libra
Ten of any suit with the page of the same suit	Scorpio
Page of any suit with the knight of the same suit	Sagittarius
Knight of any suit with the queen of the same suit	Capricorn
Queen of any suit with the king of the same suit	Star sign unknown
King of any suit with the ace of the same suit	Star sign unknown

19. Sample Question for Course

You are doing a reading for Fran and you draw seven cards. You notice that the Three of Staves is the first card, and the Four of Staves is the seventh card pulled out. Do you mention a birth month to her?

No. The cards are placed too far apart in the reading and therefore don't mean a star sign or birth month.

A. Yes. You ask if Fran knows someone born in March or April, who may actually be an Aries, but may have their birthday anywhere in March or April.
B. Yes. You ask Fran if she knows an Aries.

20. Sample Question for Course

You do a reading for Janie and you have five cards on the table. There are three cups cards, all three in a row. The Ace, Two and Three of Cups are all in Janie's reading. Do you mention a birth month?

No, it only works if there's two cards in a row for a birth month reading.

A. Yes, ask if she is aware of someone born in January, February or March.
B. Consider that January, February or March might be a significant time in Janie's life and mention this to her, including that there might be birth's during that time.
C. Both B and C are correct.

Yes, No or Maybe

If you want to know if the cards are a yes or a no, then ask your question, feel into the cards, and then choose one card.

- Even numbers are a yes.
- Odd numbers are a no.
- Court cards are a maybe.
- Spirit cards mean we're not meant to know yet.

Always ask follow up questions when asking a simple yes or no question. Follow up questions will ensure that the answer received was accurate and not a different message from spirit.

If I ask a question on behalf of a client and received a 'yes' answer to their question, I then ask another question to check that the yes is accurate. For example – Alyson asks if she will get a new job this week and I draw out an even card for her. This might be a yes. However spirit might be trying to pass on a different response, therefore I would draw another card and ask the question "how likely is it that Alyson will get a new job this month?" If the new card was the Ace of Pentacles, this denotes new career so the answer will be "yes, you will likely get a new job this month."

21. Sample Question for Course

Alyson asks if her relationship will last and you draw a card on her behalf whilst asking the question "can I have a yes/no answer please spirit around this question" and the card drawn is an even card. What do you say?

The first response from spirit is a yes, however let's draw another card and see what it is you have to do to ensure the path for your relationship stays the same as it is now.

- A. It's hard to tell as even cards often mean 'yes' to any answer, however I didn't ask the question properly and this may not be what the answer was.
- B. If nothing changes, the relationship will probably last, however remember you both have free will and can change this in the future.

CHAPTER SEVEN

The Life's Path

Each of the seventy-eight tarot cards has a separate meaning, but there is a logical flow to learning what number means what event/situation.

- The ace (one) to the ten of the tarot cards are **Numbers** cards and usually denote events.
- The **Court** cards usually denote people.
- The **Spirit** cards show the soul's journey from beginning to end.

Just as an example, consider the following made up reading with a forty year old man.

A man asked if he's in the right financial position to become a father now and you draw the Ten of Pentacles and the King of Pentacles.

If an ace (one) is the beginning of any journey, and the ten is considered the end. Likewise the page is the beginning of a learning journey and the king is the mastery of a skill.

If the man has been successful in his financial journey, then he might have the Ten or King of Pentacles. The ten being the successful completion of a long-term journey in the creation of wealth and abundance. The king always being the master is able to continue to create abundance rather than waste good fortune.

Therefore the Ten of Pentacles is describing someone who has created a strong foundation and has the ability to give food, shelter and clothing to a child. The King of Pentacles is the master of material and earthly matters, and is often called the provider. A person who is able to manage food, shelter, and clothing. Someone that's mastered wealth and abundance to the point where they may have their own business.

If this man has all his own food, shelter and clothing needs taken care of to the point where he can *give* food, shelter and clothing to others, then you can certainly be a parent.

Therefore the ultimate answer to the man would of course be: "Yes, you can have children now, what are you waiting for? You have enough to share."

If I was doing the reading for this man, I might then caution him to make sure he shows love (water,) and also spends a bit of money on things like fun (fire) and plans (air) for holidays (fire again,) as both cards drawn are earth cards, which can suggest that the man is all about work or money. Yes, he'd be able to provide for his family, but his family also need his time and his love. "The family that plays together stays together" might be something that he needs to hear.

The Numbers Cards

Let's look at the Numbers cards first. The ace (one) is obviously the beginning of a journey and the ten is obviously the end.

One is the number of beginnings, we have already created our ace cards. You might like to take a moment now to consider the ace cards that you created towards the beginning of this book.

I think of the numbers from ace to ten of the tarot cards in the same way that numerologists see our year cycles.

The one is where we have an idea. The two is where we learn how to implement the idea. The three is where we put the idea into action.

The four, five and six is the same as the one, two and three only there are more people involved. We are trying to work with others and struggling to succeed as a group. Therefore the four is where we have an idea that includes other people. The five is where we learn how to implement the idea with the group. The six is where we put the idea into motion, all working together.

The seven, eight and nine is the same as the four, five, and six however we are mastering working with others and helping those around us to work together. We are better at doing everything now. We are more responsible for others. Therefore the seven is where we have an idea that includes either family, friends or a wider group of people, which can mean more competition and friction. The eight is where we teach others and help others around us travel calmly through change. The nine is where we lead major projects to completion.

The ten is the completion of the cycle.

The table showing the flow of energy from the one through to the ten of our journeys:

	Start	Learn	Do
One - three is where we do things on our own.	One (Ace) Have an idea. Something for yourself to do, or have for yourself. It could even be a new love. We often meet our love partner in a one year.	Two Learn how to do it. We take up a course, or apprenticeship. We often get engaged, or marry. It's a time for decisions.	Three Do. We put into practice everything we learnt before. We cement our relationships, we don't know much yet and things happen unexpectedly.
Four - six is where we work alongside other people.	Four Finish off small projects, have a peaceful or romantic interlude, then have an idea. Usually this idea involves other people.	Five (the middle) Transition and change. We are working with other people, and not on our own. This can be frustrating or fun. We can make changes together.	Six Be the leader to get things done. Time to shine as an employee (or mother, or boss.) and also a time that you may be challenged by others.
Seven - nine is where we use what we've learned. We are able to help ourselves and those around us.	Seven Complete projects. Take some time off to reconnect with friends and family. This is where we step into the creation of another idea or project.	Eight We already know how to proceed, and therefore don't need to learn. Now we can teach others. This is the time to teach other people and be the mentors. Excellent for success and travel.	Nine Do. Big projects are underway which include other people. We might feel overwhelmed with how much there is to do, but we're able to manage ourselves well now if we try.
Transition to start the cycle again.	Ten Finishing off large projects. Looking back at what you've achieved over the last ten years, and then have a new idea.		

Therefore, the ace, four, seven and ten cards are related to new ideas.

An ace (one) indicates that we are working on our own, or came up with an idea on our own, or need to have a fresh start within rather than looking to others to fix anything. With an ace (one) we might have met one new person. Started a new job. Had a baby. An ace is a significant new beginning. Most new transitions start with a time out first. You may remember a time in your life where you left work and then felt that you were living in state of limbo before another opportunity presented itself. A relationship may have ended unexpectedly and you felt like you were living in limbo whilst you sorted out what to do with yourself next.

There is a saying that the universe abhors a vacuum and this means that the universe will always line something up for you to do if you're currently not doing anything. Sometimes you have to **end** what you are currently doing in order to progress.

The two, five and eight cards are all about learning and teaching. With two we are undergoing training ourselves; we are learning something new. Either a new skill, or how to be in a relationship. With five we are trying to learn how to get along with others. In a relationship, we may be trying to understand a new partner and not get upset about little differences. The eight card is where we're very knowledgeable at what we do and can now teach others.

The three, six and nine cards are all about doing! Full steam ahead! The three is us doing things for ourselves. Maybe starting our business, or cementing our relationship. Threes can indicate surprises as this is where we are busy going about our lives and other people can impact us unexpectedly. The six cards are about doing very well, usually leading the way for others, and we rarely get surprised by others. The nine is where you are the captain of projects which may be coming to a critical juncture. You have to be working and making sure everyone else is too. If a nine shows up in a reading it doesn't have to mean a career, it can mean that you have a role to play with making sure your family get on around the Christmas dinner table.

The ten indicates projects undertaken, completing or tidying up. A ten is where we consider what has been achieved and hopefully be proud of ourselves. It's where we drop that enormous burden we've been carrying so long, and it's where we take a good time out and consider the next stage of our lives. Often we put down a major project, take a break, and then, lo and behold, we start something new.

Now we are going to create our next cards.

The Twos

"Pause you who read this, and think for a moment
of the long chain of iron or gold, of thorns or flowers,
that would never have bound you, but for the
formation of the first link on one memorable day."

Charles Dickens

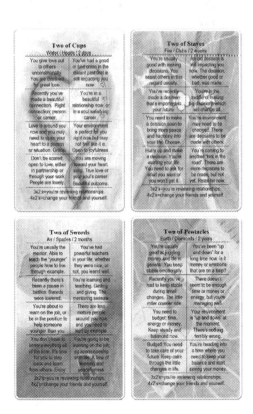

The above quote gives a good understanding of that moment in time where we choose to fall in love and marry (love/cups/water) or choose not to. We choose to do exciting adventures or not (fire/staves.) We make a right decision or a bad one (air/swords/mental ideas.) We choose to save our money or spend it all (earth/food, shelter and clothing/pentacles).

The Two is about finding balance. The Ying/Yang symbol is **only** special because it has two sides. Both have to be joined in order to find harmony. One side cannot take over from the other. There is a good or bad option, a left or right, an up or down, but there is never one without the other. The two must be in union. The point where the road forks and you have to decide.

The table showing the flow of energy from the one through to the ten of our journeys:

	Start	Learn	Do
One - three is where we do things on our own.	One (Ace) Have an idea. Something for yourself to do, or have for yourself. It could even be a new love. We often meet our love partner in a one year.	Two Learn how to do it. We take up a course, or apprenticeship. We often get engaged, or marry. It's a time for decisions.	Three Do. We put into practice everything we learnt before. We cement our relationships, we don't know much yet and things happen unexpectedly.
Four - six is where we work alongside other people.	Four Finish off small projects, have a peaceful or romantic interlude, then have an idea. Usually this idea involves other people.	Five (the middle) Transition and change. We are working with other people, and not on our own. This can be frustrating or fun. We can make changes together.	Six Be the leader to get things done. Time to shine as an employee (or mother, or boss.) and also a time that you may be challenged by others.
Seven - nine is where we use what we've learned. We are able to help ourselves and those around us.	Seven Complete projects. Take some time off to reconnect with friends and family. This is where we step into the creation of another idea or project.	Eight We already know how to proceed, and therefore don't need to learn. Now we can teach others. This is the time to teach other people and be the mentors. Excellent for success and travel.	Nine Do. Big projects are underway which include other people. We might feel overwhelmed with how much there is to do, but we're able to manage ourselves well now if we try.
Transition to start the cycle again.	Ten Finishing off large projects. Looking back at what you've achieved over the last ten years, and then have a new idea.		

Two of Cups: Loving Union

The Two of Cups indicates loving union: a marriage of hearts, not necessarily on paper. Remember this is a water element, so there is emotion involved. The Two of Cups may also indicate the perfect job in the right place, doing things that you love. This card may also imply that your love life is beautiful and that a loving union is around you. Your career, home, environment, and friends are perfect for you right now, even if it doesn't feel like it.

Two of Staves: Decisions

The Two of Staves appears in readings when decisions are required. It may be a lot of little decisions rather than one big one. Remember, this is the fire element, so there is passion and energy depicted here also. Decisions are indicated nonetheless and there is now an opportunity to choose a new direction. If in the negative, this card can imply that people are avoiding making necessary decisions. Look to the other cards in the reading spread to understand what kind of decision is required.

Two of Swords: Mentoring

The Two of Swords is the mentoring card. The mental see-saw of life where you learn, and then teach, you get and then give. This is an air card so we know we are dealing with processes of the mind. I'm in two minds. I could live in two places. I think I could do either career. This card can indicate that people need to learn from one another and can also mean that people are learning on the job e.g., an apprenticeship. This card can indicate that conflicting ideas between people (and therefore some kind of argument) has been put on hold for the time being. For instance, people put their differences aside usually on public holidays like Christmas. You may be impacted by younger or less mature people now, and this card is a reminder to mentor them rather than dictate to these people what is required. Explain the required behavior rather than coerce.

Two of Pentacles: Balance

The Two of Pentacles implies a need to budget, and maintain inner harmony and balance. This card often has the yin/yang symbol on it which means all things in harmony. This is an earth card and depicts a slower and more practical approach to life than the other twos. This card may indicate a need to save money. There may be a need to stay calm and be less emotional now. Try and remain sensible and down to earth and practical about changes in your life. The message is you need to keep your balance. Look at the balance in your life between work and home. Is there balance? Does something need to change to bring harmony back into your family? Maybe the food and drink being brought into the body is low quality. Make sure you eat and drink correctly for now.

Exercise: The Two of Cups

Look at your Two of Water/Cups/Heart card again and this time think of your own life. Write down ten examples where you have had the Two of Cups energy in your life.

1) Example: the day I married my husband. The day my baby met my elder child. When my partner and I decided to go travelling together.

_____

2)

_____

3)

_____

4)

_____

5)

_____

6)

_____

7)

_____

8)

_____

9)

_____

10)

_____

Draw your idea of what this card looks like to you.

Exercise: The Two of Staves

Look at your Two of Fire/Staves/Wands/Clubs and this time think of your own life. Write down ten examples where you have had the Two of Staves energy in your life. Don't focus on trying to be right, just go with what *feels* right for you.

1) Example: when I was at a crossroads with two different ideas of what may give me passion next. Should I take up yoga or Pilates?

_____

2)

_____

3)

_____

4)

_____

5)

_____

6)

_____

7)

_____

8)

_____

9)

_____

10)

_____

Draw your idea of what this card looks like to you.

Exercise: The Two of Swords

Look at your Two of Air/Swords/Spades card and this time think of your own life. Write down ten examples where you have had the Two of Swords energy in your life. Don't focus on trying to be right, just go with what feels right for you.

1) Example: when I didn't know which idea was right. When I fell into a mentoring relationship of learning and teaching, getting and giving.

_____

2)

_____

3)

_____

4)

_____

5)

_____

6)

_____

7)

_____

8)

_____

9)

_____

10)

_____

Draw your idea of what this card looks like to you.

Exercise: The Two of Pentacles

Look at your Two of Earth/Pentacles/Diamonds/Coins card and think of your own life. Write down ten examples where you have had the Two of Pentacles energy in your life. Don't focus on trying to be right, just go with what **feels** right for you.

1) Example: when I balanced the budget.

_____

2)

_____

3)

_____

4)

_____

5)

_____

6)

_____

7)

_____

8)

_____

9)

_____

10)

_____

Draw your idea of what this card looks like to you.

22. Sample Question for Course

Luke wants to figure out the best career that he could possibly do right now and you ask him to draw out a card and it's the Two of Swords. What do you tell him?

    A. The Two of Swords is a mentoring card, so you would make an excellent mentor right now.

    B. The Two of Swords can indicate learning on the job: you learn you teach, you get you give. Maybe try and apprenticeship where you can learn as you go.

    C. The Two of Swords can indicate that you're good with being in two minds. Perhaps try something like psychology.

    D. All of the above are correct, when joined together in one big conversation.

23. Sample Question for Course

Luke wants to know if a relationship will work out and you ask him to draw a card and he draws the Two of Cups. What do you tell him?

    A. Two's mean decisions, so it's undecided whether or not the relationship will work.

    B. The Two of Cups means two hearts joined together in loving union, so it looks like the relationship has real potential. You both have free will and therefore a choice of what happens next, however it looks great.

    C. The Two of Cups means two people travelling together, so it can indicate that you're going to travel together for a while, but probably not forever.

    D. Both B and C are right.

24. Sample Question for Course

Luke asks if he should stay in the same job that he's in now and pulls out three card. All of them are twos. The Two of Cups, the Two of Staves, and the Two of Swords. What do you tell him?

    A. You seem to be making changes in the relationships around you and making small decisions around what to do next. It looks like you want to and likely will change your uniform, peers and your environment around you, which indicates that your work will change. It looks like it's your decision though which is good. You can always change your mind if you want too and stay where you are now.

    B. The Two of Staves is the decisions card, so that means that you're going to make the decision about staying or going yourself.

    C. The decision is yours, as shown by the Two of Staves. The place you're in now is great as shown by the Two of Cups, but you have a choice to make and have two great jobs you could take.

    D. All of the above answers are right.

The Threes

"I learned this, at least, by my experiment: that if one advances confidently in the direction of his dreams, and endeavors to live the life which he has imagined, he will meet with a success unexpected in common hours."

Henry David Thoreau

Threes are power cards where we are active and busy. Threes can indicate three people involved in a relationship situation. The Holy Trilogy, the Three Musketeers, the Maiden, the Mother, and the Crone. Another example of three energy is the mother, father and new baby.

The table showing the flow of energy from the one through to the ten of our journeys:

	Start	Learn	Do
One - three is where we do things on our own.	One (Ace) Have an idea. Something for yourself to do, or have for yourself. It could even be a new love. We often meet our love partner in a one year.	Two Learn how to do it. We take up a course, or apprenticeship. We often get engaged, or marry. It's a time for decisions.	Three Do. We put into practice everything we learnt before. We cement our relationships, we don't know much yet and things happen unexpectedly.
Four - six is where we work alongside other people.	Four Finish off small projects, have a peaceful or romantic interlude, then have an idea. Usually this idea involves other people.	Five (the middle) Transition and change. We are working with other people, and not on our own. This can be frustrating or fun. We can make changes together.	Six Be the leader to get things done. Time to shine as an employee (or mother, or boss.) and also a time that you may be challenged by others.
Seven - nine is where we use what we've learned. We are able to help ourselves and those around us.	Seven Complete projects. Take some time off to reconnect with friends and family. This is where we step into the creation of another idea or project.	Eight We already know how to proceed, and therefore don't need to learn. Now we can teach others. This is the time to teach other people and be the mentors. Excellent for success and travel.	Nine Do. Big projects are underway which include other people. We might feel overwhelmed with how much there is to do, but we're able to manage ourselves well now if we try.
Transition to start the cycle again.	Ten Finishing off large projects. Looking back at what you've achieved over the last ten years, and then have a new idea.		

Three of Cups: Surprises of the Heart

Three of Cups can indicate a surprise is underway, or solace and rescue of the heart is available to you now. The type of surprise in store for you may be divined by looking at the other cards that are drawn in the reading. Some surprises are wonderful, like an engagement or an invitation. This card may also imply that you need to give gifts and surprise people. When the Three of Cups shows up you might be getting good news which can take any form, for example, a wedding invitation.

Three of Staves: Success

The Three of Staves is the success card. This card shows that people are being successful in their own right. This card can mean that people don't need to work as a team, as they're now capable of achieving their own goals. The advice of this card is to be successful, regardless of what's happening around you now. It doesn't matter what other people think, do, or say, it's time to shine! Proceed through life with a big smile and a winning attitude!

Three of Swords: Division and Separation

The Three of Swords can indicate division, separation and heartbreak. Every change in life comes with a form of loss. People have to leave a job in order to get a better job. Some relationships dissolve in order for a better relationship to come about. Sometimes it can be heartbreaking to leave a place, however leaving has to take place in order to move to a better place. This card may mean that mediation is required and that you are speaking a different love language to your partner. Are three people involved in your relationship? This card may indicate that a well-meaning friend or family member is actually making a relationship situation worse rather than better. Sometimes advice needs to come from specialists! Generally "three is a crowd" is the statement now for all relationships. The mind has come before the heart in this situation, and sometimes that's a good thing.

Three of Pentacles: Perfectionism

This strong and stable earth card shows people want to do the very best. As this card is a doing card in the earth element, it may indicate people wanting to purchase property. The Three of Pentacles implies perfectionism. If you are a perfectionist, then you may get wonderful things done each day and feel very proud of yourself, or you may never start anything as it won't be perfect, so why bother? The message if you've received the Three of Pentacles is near enough is sometimes good enough and just get the job done. This card can mean that everything is perfect, or that people are being too harsh on themselves and everyone around them now. People need to remember that nothing is ever going to be the way I want it to be, so I will aim to do it the best I can, rather than make it perfect. Life will be easier if people try not to judge things around themselves too harshly.

Exercise: The Three of Cups

Look at your Three of Water/Cups/Heart card again and this time think of your own life. Write down ten examples where you have had the Three of Cups energy in your life.

1) Example: the day I sent out wedding invitations to people I love, so that they could come to my wedding. The day I sent a bunch of flowers to a friend. The day that I found out that the person I was in a relationship with, is a different person than who I thought they were.

_____

2)

_____

3)

_____

4)

_____

5)

_____

6)

_____

7)

_____

8)

_____

9)

_____

10)

_____

Draw your idea of what this card looks like to you.

Exercise: The Three of Staves

Look at your Three of Fire/Staves/Wands/Clubs card and this time think of your own life. Write down ten examples where you have had the Three of Staves energy in your life.

1) Example: when I started singing, or dancing classes and did well at them. When I opened my business.

_____

2)

_____

3)

_____

4)

_____

5)

_____

6)

_____

7)

_____

8)

_____

9)

_____

10)

_____

Draw your idea of what this card looks like to you.

Exercise: The Three of Swords

Look at your Three of Air/Swords/Spades card and this time think of your own life. Write down ten examples where you have had the Three of Swords energy in your life.

1) Example: when we moved house. When we divorced. When we went to mediation to assist our marriage. The day we got back together again.

_____

2)
_____

3)
_____

4)
_____

5)
_____

6)
_____

7)
_____

8)
_____

9)
_____

10)
_____

Draw your idea of what this card looks like to you.

Exercise: The Three of Pentacles

Look at your Three of Earth/Pentacles/Diamonds/Coins card and think of your own life. Write down ten examples where you have had the Three of Pentacles energy in your life.

1) Example: when we signed the contract on our home. When I decided to put into practice all of those things that make me feel better physically, e.g., exercise.

_____

2)

_____

3)

_____

4)

_____

5)

_____

6)

_____

7)

_____

8)

_____

9)

_____

10)

_____

Draw your idea of what this card looks like to you.

25. Sample Question for Course

Andrew says he isn't doing well at work and wants to know how his boss feels about him. He draws the Three of Staves. What do you tell him?

A. The Three of Staves is actually a success card. Are you sure they don't like you? Maybe you're just feeling like you're not at your potential and judging yourself quite harshly?

B. I'm not allowed to read for others without their permission, however it looks like spirit is telling you that you're doing better than you think you are. The Three of Staves is a success card.

C. Both A and C combined are an appropriate answer.

D. All of the above are wrong.

26. Sample Question for Course

Andrew asks for a future reading and the Three of Swords is showing in the happening next position in the reading. What do you say about that?

A. Remember this is just a reading, and life can change because of the decisions we make. It looks like you're about to undergo a change. Like you're deciding to move on from a situation or place or person. The Three of Swords indicates separation and can feel a little sad. Perhaps you'll decide to leave a house you love in order to purchase a house that better suits your family's needs.

B. The Three of Swords indicates separation, sadness and loss. It looks like you need to take a stand and tell everyone around you how you feel in order to make everything stay the way it is now.

C. Relationships that are working will continue to work, however the Three of Swords can indicate that a change is required in order to make relationships better. It could be that you need to go to meditation, or it could be a simple as a change of home or job that's being discussed in your immediate future. Stay open to suggestions for change and improvement now.

D. Both A and C are appropriate, however more cards are required to see what type of energy is coming in with the Three of Swords. I'd ask him to draw more cards.

The Fours

"The best love is the kind that awakens the soul and makes us reach for more, that plants a fire in our hearts and brings peace to our minds. And that's what you've given me. That's what I'd hoped to give you forever"

Nicholas Sparks

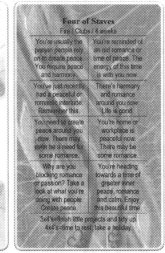

The table showing the flow of energy from the one through to the ten of our journeys:

	Start	Learn	Do
One - three is where we do things on our own.	One (Ace) Have an idea. Something for yourself to do, or have for yourself. It could even be a new love. We often meet our love partner in a one year.	Two Learn how to do it. We take up a course, or apprenticeship. We often get engaged, or marry. It's a time for decisions.	Three Do. We put into practice everything we learnt before. We cement our relationships, we don't know much yet and things happen unexpectedly.
Four - six is where we work alongside other people.	Four Finish off small projects, have a peaceful or romantic interlude, then have an idea. Usually this idea involves other people.	Five (the middle) Transition and change. We are working with other people, and not on our own. This can be frustrating or fun. We can make changes together.	Six Be the leader to get things done. Time to shine as an employee (or mother, or boss.) and also a time that you may be challenged by others.
Seven - nine is where we use what we've learned. We are able to help ourselves and those around us.	Seven Complete projects. Take some time off to reconnect with friends and family. This is where we step into the creation of another idea or project.	Eight We already know how to proceed, and therefore don't need to learn. Now we can teach others. This is the time to teach other people and be the mentors. Excellent for success and travel.	Nine Do. Big projects are underway which include other people. We might feel overwhelmed with how much there is to do, but we're able to manage ourselves well now if we try.
Transition to start the cycle again.	Ten Finishing off large projects. Looking back at what you've achieved over the last ten years, and then have a new idea.		

Four of Cups: A Healing Timeout from Relationships

You may need a rest from a relationship, or a short time out is on the way for you. Relationships are confusing now. A short break in relating to others may be required to clear the air before a feeling of calm can come once again. The Four of Cups can indicate some frustration in relating to others, but little steps that can be taken which can bring healing into relationships. This card asks that you relax and don't make rash decisions regarding relationships now. Also, maybe take some time out alone to decide what you need to do about your relationships. When this card appears, people are confused and unsure of which direction to take. This is the card of mixed emotions. If this card was pulled out for a question around someone's career, then they may be unhappy in one job, preferring to volunteer, or contract, to fulfil their need to move and change.

Four of Staves: Peace and Romance

The Four of Staves is the card of peace, harmony and romance. Romance doesn't have to be between two lovers. Romantic feelings can be stirred when we're reviewing our history, the romance of the years. This card can indicate a period of peace and it can also indicate that people are warm and loving. This card always reflects calm, or a short break away with a loved one, a romantic weekend perhaps. Emotions are joyful and peace and contentment are available when this card appears. This is a doing (fire) card, so it does indicate that you may have to do something in order to create peace, for instance you might have to move house, or change jobs, in order to feel happier.

Four of Swords: Rest and Recover

The Four of Swords always means rest, retreat and recover. This card usually indicates a period of respite for everyone involved, a nurturing time of calm, but the calm may be short lived! This may indicate actual rest that needs to be taken if people are tired, or recovering from illness. It should also mean that battle swords need to be put away for a while as everyone needs to take a breath and come back later when everything has calmed down a bit. This card implies that people need time out to recover; this may mean that people need to take a short trip away by themselves. Take a break, go on retreat, you deserve it! This could mean a short hospital stay.

Four of Pentacles: Slow and Steady

The Four of Pentacles implies that everything is coming together slowly. You are advancing every day steadily and calmly. This card may also indicate an emotional blockage related to finances. This card can mean that you are experiencing poverty consciousness at this time. For example, if someone has four coins and they hold onto them too tightly, then they may have poverty consciousness and be miserly. Conversely they may have very little money and can't help but spend it all and then feel guilty about it later. This can apply to relationships as well. Are the relationships in your life steady and comfortable, or do you feel like you don't have enough of everything? Take every day as it comes. Be practical and pragmatic. Try not to be a spendthrift and also try not to overspend. Maybe a little bit of savings each week is required right now. In relationships everything is coming together and there is slow and steady improvement if you want the relationship to improve.

Exercise: The Four of Cups

Look at your Four of Water/Cups/Heart card again and this time think of your own life. Write down ten examples where you have had the Four of Cups energy in your life.

1) Example: when I decided to take a break from my relationship, or we had a short break away together on a little holiday. When I realized that I needed to be a better friend. When I decided to mix up my life a bit and do contract work.

_____

2)

_____

3)

_____

4)

_____

5)

_____

6)

_____

7)

_____

8)

_____

9)

_____

10)

_____

Draw your idea of what this card looks like to you.

Exercise - The Four of Staves

Look at your Four of Fire/Staves/Wands/Clubs and this time think of your own life. Write down ten examples where you have had the Four of Staves energy in your life.

1) Example: when I moved and felt so much happier. When my partner and I went away for a short romantic holiday.

_____

2)

_____

3)

_____

4)

_____

5)

_____

6)

_____

7)

_____

8)

_____

9)

_____

10)

_____

Draw your idea of what this card looks like to you.

Exercise - The Four of Swords

Look at your Four of Air/Swords/Spades card and this time think of your own life. Write down ten examples where you have had the Four of Swords energy in your life.

1) Example: when I went on a healing retreat. When I went into hospital for that small operation for a day. When I decided to let time and distance heal a relationship.

2)

3)

4)

5)

6)

7)

8)

9)

10)

Draw your idea of what this card looks like to you.

Exercise - The Four of Pentacles

Look at your Four of Earth/Pentacles/Diamonds/Coins card and think of your own life. Write down ten examples where you have had the Four of Pentacles energy in your life.

1) Example: when I realized that I was too focused on money.

_____

2)

_____

3)

_____

4)

_____

5)

_____

6)

_____

7)

_____

8)

_____

9)

_____

10)

_____

Draw your idea of what this card looks like to you.

27. Sample Question for Course

Bernadette has a health scare and is asking if she will be ok. The Four of Swords is drawn. What do you tell her?

    A. The Four of Swords can reflect that a time out is required. You might need a good long rest.

    B. The Four of Swords can reflect that a time out is required. You might need to quit your job and stay at home for four months.

    C. The Four of Swords can reflect that a time out is required. You might end up in hospital, but you'll be ok.

    D. The Four of Swords can reflect that a time out is required. You might need a space to heal and recover, and this might mean a short hospital stay or tests. Go about the tests calmly.

28. Sample Question for Course

Bernadette is confused about a relationship and draws the Four of Cups. What do you tell her?

    A. The Four of Cups is confusion in relationships, so basically the cards are agreeing that there is supposed to be confusion right now. Don't worry, this time will pass.

    B. The Four of Cups can denote a time out in existing relationships. You may like to have a weekend apart or there may be another time out happening in the relationship right now.

    C. The Four of Cups shows confusion, perhaps we need to draw more cards to show what your advice is, and what your partner's advice is.

    D. All of the above are accurate.

The Fives

"Life is an opportunity, benefit from it.
Life is beauty, admire it.
Life is a dream, realize it.
Life is a challenge, meet it.
Life is a duty, complete it.
Life is a game, play it.
Life is a promise, fulfill it.
Life is sorrow, overcome it.
Life is a song, sing it.
Life is a struggle, accept it.
Life is a tragedy, confront it.
Life is an adventure, dare it.
Life is luck, make it.
Life is too precious, do not destroy it.
Life is life, fight for it."

Mother Teresa

The table showing the flow of energy from the one through to the ten of our journeys:

	Start	Learn	Do
One - three is where we do things on our own.	One (Ace) Have an idea. Something for yourself to do, or have for yourself. It could even be a new love. We often meet our love partner in a one year.	Two Learn how to do it. We take up a course, or apprenticeship. We often get engaged, or marry. It's a time for decisions.	Three Do. We put into practice everything we learnt before. We cement our relationships, we don't know much yet and things happen unexpectedly.
Four - six is where we work alongside other people.	Four Finish off small projects, have a peaceful or romantic interlude, then have an idea. Usually this idea involves other people.	Five (the middle) Transition and change. We are working with other people, and not on our own. This can be frustrating or fun. We can make changes together.	Six Be the leader to get things done. Time to shine as an employee (or mother, or boss.) and also a time that you may be challenged by others.
Seven - nine is where we use what we've learned. We are able to help ourselves and those around us.	Seven Complete projects. Take some time off to reconnect with friends and family. This is where we step into the creation of another idea or project.	Eight We already know how to proceed, and therefore don't need to learn. Now we can teach others. This is the time to teach other people and be the mentors. Excellent for success and travel.	Nine Do. Big projects are underway which include other people. We might feel overwhelmed with how much there is to do, but we're able to manage ourselves well now if we try.
Transition to start the cycle again.	Ten Finishing off large projects. Looking back at what you've achieved over the last ten years, and then have a new idea.		

Five of Cups: the Cup is Half Full

The emotional cup is half full or half empty depending on how you're looking at your life from moment to moment. When the Five of Cups appears in a reading you are asked to look at life as it is and not cry over what's missing. This card can indicate a deep sadness, however with the five cups, two cups are usually full and three are spilt. The message is always try to appreciate what you have. The Five of Cups implies people crying due to the passing of a loved one, the end of a relationship, or another tragedy. There may be a person that's missing.

For example, if a beloved son has moved out of home and left the place feeling empty. There may be insecurity in relationships now, as this card indicates that the relationship isn't fantastic, but it's not terrible either. You can improve relationships or make them worse, it's up to you. If the question was around career, then your job may be ok for now, however it might be time to start looking around. There may be major things missing that are required to get your job done, and it may be a person or special equipment that is absent. If the question is around the current living situation, then it needs improving as it may be creating negativity and chaos. At the very least, a clean-up is required.

Five of Staves: Details

The Five of Staves indicates the hurdles of everyday life and that people need to take care of the details. It can also mean that people are not enjoying taking care of the details and doing sloppy work, resulting in problems later on. Either way, the details and those annoying little jobs have to be done. You may as well do them all happily and do them all well! If the small jobs aren't done, then they will become big problems later.

Five of Swords: Where to Next?

The Five of Swords indicates confusion around direction. Fives are in the middle between the ace of new beginnings and the ten of completions. If people are in the middle of making plans, then they may not know where to go next or what to do next. Being uncertain about a career path, or relationship, or living situation can be stressful, however this stage of life is necessary for all of us. This card indicates that if people don't know where to go next and what to do next, then they can go anywhere and do anything! This is the card of opportunity if viewed from this perspective. If this card has shown up then spirit is asking you to review your life plans and consider changing job, or home, or perhaps in living overseas for a while.

Five of Pentacles: We Have Enough

The Five of Pentacles implies that you have enough of everything but that you might not feel like you do. The abundance cup is half full and therefore half empty. Abundance is food, shelter, clothing and love. If this card has shown up in your reading, you are being reminded to be grateful for what you do have and not focus too much on what you don't have. You can improve your situation, and there is change taking place now. This may indicate that the workplace or career is changing. Be grateful for what you have and build upon it. Life may be changing, and people may be feeling some friction. Don't be drawn into becoming negative or argumentative.

Exercise: The Five of Cups

Look at your Five of Water/Cups/Heart card again and this time think of your own life. Write down ten examples where you have had the Five of Cups energy in your life.

1) Example: when I felt sad about losing my friend. When I realized I would have to leave the job that I loved. When I decided to look at the bright side of life.

_____

2)

_____

3)

_____

4)

_____

5)

_____

6)

_____

7)

_____

8)

_____

9)

_____

10)

_____

Draw your idea of what this card looks like to you.

Exercise: The Five of Staves

Look at your Five of Fire/Staves/Wands/Clubs and this time think of your own life. Write down ten examples where you have had the Five of Staves energy in your life.

1) Example: when I struggled with a particular situation. When I really looked at the details of my life and analyzed what I wanted to change.

_____

2)

_____

3)

_____

4)

_____

5)

_____

6)

_____

7)

_____

8)

_____

9)

_____

10)

_____

Draw your idea of what this card looks like to you.

Exercise: The Five of Swords

Look at your Five of Air/Swords/Spades card and this time think of your own life. Write down ten examples where you have had the Five of Swords energy in your life.

1) Example: when I decided that I could live anywhere in the world if I wanted too.

_____

2)

_____

3)

_____

4)

_____

5)

_____

6)

_____

7)

_____

8)

_____

9)

_____

10)

_____

Draw your idea of what this card looks like to you.

Exercise: The Five of Pentacles

Look at your Five of Earth/Pentacles/Diamonds/Coins card and think of your own life. Write down ten examples where you have had the Five of Pentacles energy in your life.

1) Example: when I was careful with my money, time and energy. When I decided to do shift work. When I decided to change my life to make a better balance between work and life/family.

_____

2)

_____

3)

_____

4)

_____

5)

_____

6)

_____

7)

_____

8)

_____

9)

_____

10)

_____

Draw your idea of what this card looks like to you.

29. Sample Question for Course

Ken asks about his work and whether he should stay in his current role or move to another role. He draws the Five of Swords. Both answers below are right, which one is the **most** right?

    A. The Five of Swords can indicate that the sky's the limit. If you wanted to work overseas right now, you could. If you wanted to work at a fly in / fly out job, you could. When this card shows up you need a change. The time is right.

    B. The Five of Swords indicates that you could go anywhere and do anything right now, especially if you've been going round and round in circles trying to figure out what to do next. It's time to have a think about your future and consider making a change. Don't block yourself.

30. Sample Question for Course

Ken wants to know what's happening with his friendship circle and he draws three cards, all fives. What do you tell him?

    A. Fives are all transition cards, and as you've drawn all fives, it appears that your friendship circle is changing, it could be that the same people continue to be around you but you'll find that the energy of the group might change.

    B. Fives can indicate frustration and challenges, friendships may be hard work now. Try not to create any unnecessary conflict as too many little transitions can cause tension arguments.

    C. Both A and B are right.

    D. Fives indicate transition, let everyone go around you now.

The Sixes

"If the world were merely seductive, that would be easy. If it were merely challenging, that would be no problem. But I arise in the morning torn between a desire to improve the world and a desire to enjoy the world. This makes it hard to plan the day."

E.B. White

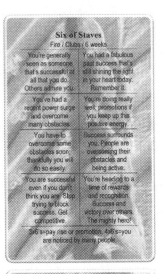

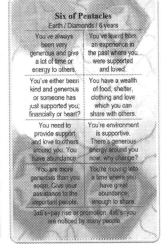

The table showing the flow of energy from the one through to the ten of our journeys:

	Start	Learn	Do
One - three is where we do things on our own.	One (Ace) Have an idea. Something for yourself to do, or have for yourself. It could even be a new love. We often meet our love partner in a one year.	Two Learn how to do it. We take up a course, or apprenticeship. We often get engaged, or marry. It's a time for decisions.	Three Do. We put into practice everything we learnt before. We cement our relationships, we don't know much yet and things happen unexpectedly.
Four - six is where we work alongside other people.	Four Finish off small projects, have a peaceful or romantic interlude, then have an idea. Usually this idea involves other people.	Five (the middle) Transition and change. We are working with other people, and not on our own. This can be frustrating or fun. We can make changes together.	Six Be the leader to get things done. Time to shine as an employee (or mother, or boss.) and also a time that you may be challenged by others.
Seven - nine is where we use what we've learned. We are able to help ourselves and those around us.	Seven Complete projects. Take some time off to reconnect with friends and family. This is where we step into the creation of another idea or project.	Eight We already know how to proceed, and therefore don't need to learn. Now we can teach others. This is the time to teach other people and be the mentors. Excellent for success and travel.	Nine Do. Big projects are underway which include other people. We might feel overwhelmed with how much there is to do, but we're able to manage ourselves well now if we try.
Transition to start the cycle again.	Ten Finishing off large projects. Looking back at what you've achieved over the last ten years, and then have a new idea.		

Six of Cups: Waters of Remembrance

The Six of Cups is a card of reunions and emotional memories connected to the past - the waters of remembrance. This card may indicate romance of all kinds. Romantic feelings can be held around a vehicle that has been lovingly restored and kept for years, or a place that you grew up in. When this cards shows up try not to let what's happened in the past hold you back now. You are being impacted by an emotional connection you still have from the past, if a person, perhaps you have been unable to get over a breakup from long ago. If it's about a place, perhaps you still have emotional ties to it.

Emotional attachments from the past can create beautiful: reunions and happy hours reminiscing about how things used to be. Living in the past however, will never take you forward in life. It might be time to release the emotions from the past. Remember an event from the past and say to yourself when that happened it was great or when that happened I was devastated, but remove any emotions that come up around what's happened long ago. Releasing yourself of the emotional attachment doesn't take away the memory. Tell yourself that was then, and this is now and move on. It might be time to clear the mental clutter from long ago.

Do you have items of intrinsic value that have been collected over the years? It's lovely when people give us gifts, and it's lovely when we collect mementos. It's nice to look at an object and remember when, and why, we received it. Do you need everything that you have now though? Objects may have an emotion attached to them, but throwing out the old doesn't mean throwing out the memory. It's ok to pass on the items that have been given to you to a person that needs it more.

Consider a clean out of your heart and home, but if you really love it, keep it.

Six of Staves: Victory

The Six of Staves is a challenge and victory card. This card shows overcoming hurdles or competitions of all kinds. This card can mean that your passion is returning and things are starting to move again after a period of stagnation. This card indicates interviews and rewards and recognition within the workplace. There may also be an adversary around you as this card does indicate serious competition.

Six of Swords: Science and Air Travel

The Six of Swords indicates travel or a scientific mind. Clarity of thought and good plans are associated with this card. The confusion of the Five of Swords has now passed and positive planning is taking place for all concerned. This card indicates movement and change through well thought out decisions and this leads to positive change for all concerned. If the question is regarding career, then clever ideas and quick thinking will be rewarded. If the Six of Swords shows up in the same reading as the Eight of Staves, then overseas travel is indicated.

Six of Pentacles: Enough to Share

The Six of Pentacles implies that you either have enough food, shelter, clothing and/or love to give to others, or that you are being provided for in all ways. This is the card of generosity. This card can indicate that money is being lent, which may imply success if asking for assistance from financial institutions e.g., having your loan approved. There might be a reminder to be more supportive and give your help to others. There is definitely enough of everything to go around and abundance is available to everyone.

Exercise: The Six of Cups

Look at your Six of Water/Cups/Heart card again and this time think of your own life. Write down ten examples where you have had the Six of Cups energy in your life.

1) Example: when I went to the reunion and connected up with all those people from my past. When I felt happiness and completeness for no particular reason.

2)

3)

4)

5)

6)

7)

8)

9)

10)

Draw your idea of what this card looks like to you.

Exercise: The Six of Staves

Look at your Six of Fire/Staves/Wands/Clubs card and this time think of your own life. Write down ten examples where you have had the Six of Staves energy in your life.

1) Example: when I realized how fierce the competition was and how I had to step up and do something great. When I overcame my illness.

_____

2)

_____

3)

_____

4)

_____

5)

_____

6)

_____

7)

_____

8)

_____

9)

_____

10)

_____

Draw your idea of what this card looks like to you.

Exercise: The Six of Swords

Look at your Six of Air/Swords/Spades card and this time think of your own life. Write down ten examples where you have had the Six of Swords energy in your life.

1) Example: when I chose to travel overseas. When I sought scientific help with my illness or situation. When I thought scientifically.

_____

2)

_____

3)

_____

4)

_____

5)

_____

6)

_____

7)

_____

8)

_____

9)

_____

10)

_____

Draw your idea of what this card looks like to you.

Exercise: The Six of Pentacles

Look at your Six of Earth/Pentacles/Diamonds/Coins card and think of your own life. Write down ten examples where you have had the Six of Pentacles energy in your life.

1) Example: when I had enough to give and share and I wanted to help those around me. When I got that loan from the bank.

_____

2)
_____

3)
_____

4)
_____

5)
_____

6)
_____

7)
_____

8)
_____

9)
_____

10)
_____

Draw your idea of what this card looks like to you.

31. Sample Question for Course

Kate wants to go into a festival and compete to be the festival queen. You ask what her chances of becoming queen of the festival are, and ask Kate to draw one card. The card is the Six of Staves. What do you tell her?

A. The Six of Staves shows that there is a lot of competition and potential success for you, but not guaranteed.
B. The Six of Staves is a success card, and you'll likely win.
C. Neither are correct.

32. Sample Question for Course

Kate said she'd like to meet someone and draws the Six of Cups. What do you tell her?

A. The Six of Cups is a happy card and indicates reunions. This means that you'll likely meet someone who is either from your home town, or someone that you already know.
B. The Six of Cups shows reunions and reflects meeting someone who is similar to you - a soul mate is coming into your life.
C. The Six of Cups shows that you are meant to be happy and release everything from your past and move forward in life. Expect someone new to come into your life, someone that you've never met before.

The Sevens

"My dear young cousin, if there's one thing I've learned over the eons, it's that you can't give up on your family, no matter how tempting they make it."

Rick Riordan

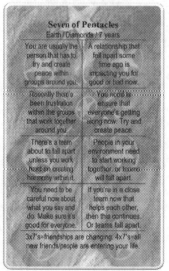

Seven of Cups
Water / Hearts / 7 days

You believe in magic and try to remain open to mystery. You make your own joy.	A relationship that happened long ago still impacts you. Healing past hurts is required now.
Recently you've become sad, or disillusioned with people around you. Disappointment.	You're feeling a little disillusioned with life right now. Everything good seems a fantasy.
You need to clear up any confusion around you as soon as you can. Things are good.	The people around you are disappointing you and are not doing what you need.
It's not a fantasy! If things appear well, then just enjoy it without questioning everything.	You might not like where you end up with relationships. There may be trouble brewing.

3x7's=friendships are changing. 4x7's=all new friends/people are entering your life.

Seven of Staves
Fire / Clubs / 7 weeks

You're a born leader and always seem to win at everything you put your mind too.	You had to "lead the way" in the past. You learnt how to take what you need in life.
Recently you had to compete with others for things you really want. Taken a stand.	You are strong and successful now, overcoming the obstacles in your life. Victory!
You're about to have victory over others. Good opportunities for advancement.	Other people may be trying to tell you what to do, or are trying to be superior to you.
You may not feel like doing this but you need to take a stand and tell others your needs.	You're stepping into a leadership role where you have power over others. Be kind.

3x7's=friendships are changing. 4x7's=all new friends/people are entering your life.

Seven of Swords
Air / Spades / 7 months

You're usually the person everyone looks towards for fortitude, hope and courage. Bravery.	You've learnt that praise and support is a powerful tool to use when dealing with others.
Recently you have felt a surge of courage. Recent strategising and thoughtfulness.	You are hopeful and are showing other people around you how they can get along.
You need to show others how to stay hopeful and brave and think through things. Courage!	You can rely on the people around you now. They want what's best and right for you.
You have fortitude, hope and courage. Why aren't you showing this right now? Be brave.	You're moving into a hopeful phase of your life; showing leadership through brilliant ideas.

3x7's=friendships are changing. 4x7's=all new friends/people are entering your life.

Seven of Pentacles
Earth / Diamonds / 7 years

You are usually the person that has to try and create peace within groups around you.	A relationship that fell apart some time ago is impacting you for good or bad now.
Recently there's been frustration within the groups that work together around you.	You need to ensure that everyone's getting along now. Try and create peace.
There's a team about to fall apart unless you work hard on creating harmony within it.	People in your environment need to start working together, or teams will fall apart.
You need to be careful now about what you say and do. Make sure it's good for everyone.	If you're in a close team now that helps each other, then this continues. Or teams fall apart.

3x7's=friendships are changing. 4x7's=all new friends/people are entering your life.

The table showing the flow of energy from the one through to the ten of our journeys:

	Start	Learn	Do
One - three is where we do things on our own.	One (Ace) Have an idea. Something for yourself to do, or have for yourself. It could even be a new love. We often meet our love partner in a one year.	Two Learn how to do it. We take up a course, or apprenticeship. We often get engaged, or marry. It's a time for decisions.	Three Do. We put into practice everything we learnt before. We cement our relationships, we don't know much yet and things happen unexpectedly.
Four - six is where we work alongside other people.	Four Finish off small projects, have a peaceful or romantic interlude, then have an idea. Usually this idea involves other people.	Five (the middle) Transition and change. We are working with other people, and not on our own. This can be frustrating or fun. We can make changes together.	Six Be the leader to get things done. Time to shine as an employee (or mother, or boss.) and also a time that you may be challenged by others.
Seven - nine is where we use what we've learned. We are able to help ourselves and those around us.	Seven Complete projects. Take some time off to reconnect with friends and family. This is where we step into the creation of another idea or project.	Eight We already know how to proceed, and therefore don't need to learn. Now we can teach others. This is the time to teach other people and be the mentors. Excellent for success and travel.	Nine Do. Big projects are underway which include other people. We might feel overwhelmed with how much there is to do, but we're able to manage ourselves well now if we try.
Transition to start the cycle again.	Ten Finishing off large projects. Looking back at what you've achieved over the last ten years, and then have a new idea.		

Seven of Cups: Create Happiness

The Seven of Cups indicates that people are feeling like everything is a fantasy. Fantasy can be wonderful if it's magical and beautiful, but a fantasy can also be quite harsh when viewed by the light of day. This card might indicate that people are feeling disillusioned and disappointed with life and the people around them. This card may also imply that there is a need to believe in magic and that things turn out the best for everyone eventually. It also can mean that friends and family have been disappointing and feelings have been hurt. Hopefully this card is implying that there is a readiness to open hearts and minds to the possibility of magic. Become sensitive to other people's feelings and to our own emotional needs now. This card can indicate that there is insecurity and an inability to trust other people.

Seven of Staves: Be Victorious

The Seven of Staves is the success and leadership card. This card shows up in readings if people are being too pushy and others are feeling overwhelmed by them. Or if people need to take a stand and show others the way to lead a better life. If this card is drawn in a reading it may be the time to let other people what your boundaries are. This card indicates success at interviews and a need to be the leader within the workplace, or in business.

Seven of Swords: Be Hopeful

The Seven of Swords is the card of hope and courage. This card can indicate that friends or co-workers need an emotional boost. This is the card of people thinking from the perspective of how they can work better with, and/or help others. The Seven of Swords reminds us of a different kind of leadership. This is now a time to be thoughtful and considerate whilst maintaining a business-like attitude. This card indicates that people are able to prove themselves in front of others now through their calm and clear thinking ability. If there are people making an emotional mess right now, stay calm and try not to feel it too much, the clear thinker is required now. Provide support and hope to others without taking away their life lessons. Lead others through their challenges by helping them make decisions, but don't make the decisions for them.

Seven of Pentacles: Be a Team Player

The Seven of Pentacles can mean that people are working together very well to build wealth. This is the card of teamwork, and conversely this card can be a warning that unless people do work together, teams and friendships may fall apart. This card indicates a need to work with others, and not alone now. For instance, if the question is about starting a new business and becoming the boss, then the answer is that other people are required to be involved. This card may indicate that there is a need to ensure all people are working together now. It may be hard to create any kind of improvement without working with other people now. There may be friction within groups of people in the environment, and you are being advised that if you can't assist matters then to try and remove yourself from the friction of it.

Exercise: The Seven of Cups

Look at your Seven of Water/Cups/Heart card again and this time think of your own life. Write down ten examples where you have had the Seven of Cups energy in your life.

1) Example: when I felt a little bit disappointed with friends or family. When I thought that the world was a magical place. When I realized that I had made a poor decision.

_____

2)

_____

3)

_____

4)

_____

5)

_____

6)

_____

7)

_____

8)

_____

9)

_____

10)

_____

Draw your idea of what this card looks like to you.

Exercise: The Seven of Staves

Look at your Seven of Fire/Staves/Wands/Clubs and this time think of your own life. Write down ten examples where you have had the Seven of Staves energy in your life.

1) Example: when I stood my ground and told people what I really thought. When I was successful with the interview and got the job. When I was a team leader.

_____

2)

_____

3)

_____

4)

_____

5)

_____

6)

_____

7)

_____

8)

_____

9)

_____

10)

_____

Draw your idea of what this card looks like to you.

Exercise: The Seven of Swords

Look at your Seven of Air/Swords/Spades card and this time think of your own life. Write down ten examples where you have had the Seven of Swords energy in your life.

1) Example: when I chose to be more hopeful about my friends and family situation. When I helped people feel more hopeful at a troubling time.

2)

3)

4)

5)

6)

7)

8)

9)

10)

Draw your idea of what this card looks like to you.

Exercise: The Seven of Pentacles

Look at your Seven of Earth/Pentacles/Diamonds/Coins card and think of your own life. Write down ten examples where you have had the Seven of Pentacles energy in your life.

1) Example: when I had to overcome a physical challenge. When I decided that I would proceed with caution with a new financial idea.

2)

3)

4)

5)

6)

7)

8)

9)

10)

Draw your idea of what this card looks like to you.

33. Sample Question for Course

Sarah wants to know if she'd be successful with her new job and she draws the Seven of Pentacles. What do you tell her?

A. The seven is all about family and friends – the job will feel like family.

B. Sevens indicate family and friends, and pentacles is abundance – wealth including food, shelter, clothing and love, and therefore money to bring in that abundance. The job will be lucrative.

C. Sevens are family and friendship, and pentacles can mean work and abundance. It may be an effort to bring people close together on the job, but if you have the intention of working as a team, and helping others to work as a team, then you'll do well.

D. None of the above are accurate.

34. Sample Question for Course

Sarah wants to travel and have fun, but people are telling her to apply for work. Sarah draws the Seven of Staves card. What do you tell her?

A. Sevens can indicate friends and family, and the Seven of Staves is a challenge card. Often associated with victory in all challenges. It's time to apply for and win that job.

B. Sevens can indicate friends and family, and the Seven of Staves is a challenge card. Often associated with victory in all challenges. It's time to stand up for what you believe in and do what you want.

C. Both A and B are right.

D. Sevens can indicate friends and family, and the Seven of Staves is a challenge card. Often associated with victory in all challenges. We need to draw more cards to see the outcome of staying and applying for the job, or travelling, knowing that you can overcome any challenges in your path now.

The Eights

"We are travelers on a cosmic journey, stardust, swirling and dancing in the eddies and whirlpools of infinity. Life is eternal. We have stopped for a moment to encounter each other, to meet, to love, to share. This is a precious moment. It is a little parenthesis in eternity."

Paulo Coelho

Eight of Cups
Water / Hearts / 8 days

Meditation and connection to spirit is something that should be very important to you.	There's surrender and release in your past. You learnt to just give up and let go. Is that good?
You've either been avoiding reality or have had to release someone or something	Good escapism (movies/books) and/or meditation required now. Travel planning.
You're going to have to learn how to "surrender and release" soon. Let go and move on.	It's hard to tell what's happening around you now, surrender and release your fears.
Focus on reality, try and surrender any idea or goal that you had and accept what is.	A situation is coming where you release your fears. You are getting ready to move on.

3x8's=Travel plans changing. 4x8's=Your life plans are about to change for good.

Eight of Staves
Fire / Clubs / 8 weeks

You usually act fast. You've had many changes in life and have no difficulty with them.	Sudden moves and changes that you've done in the past are impacting you now.
You've just had lightning fast ideas or changes taking place. You were unable to stop.	Sudden movement. Sudden activity. Everything's changing so fast. Speed up!
Very fast changes about to occur. You may wish for a slower pace, but speed up anyway.	There's lightning fast changes being made around you now. Just try and keep up with them.
You need to speed up or be left behind. You may have to consider travel or healing.	You're heading towards a time where you make changes quickly. Overseas travel?

3x8's=Travel plans changing. 4x8's=Your life plans are about to change for good.

Eight of Swords
Air / Spades / 8 months

You're usually able to self-heal and manipulate circumstances or people to suit you.	You've had to go through an inner healing journey in the past and have healing abilities.
You've just been through a time of healing on the inside. Lighter thoughts came in.	Healing time for you right now. Try not to manipulate others, or yourself, into false beliefs.
You need to go on an internal healing journey soon. Changes to take place on the inside.	People around you are unwell, or are trying to coerce or manipulate you for good or for ill.
You need to heal yourself and stop thinking other people are the cause of any issue.	An inner healing journey is coming. A time to reflect on your life and decide on the next stage.

3x8's=Travel plans changing. 4x8's=Your life plans are about to change for good.

Eight of Pentacles
Earth / Diamonds / 8 years

You've always come easily into positions of knowledge and teaching others	You remember a time when you felt great about who you were, and what you achieved.
Recently you've helped others by imparting wisdom that you've learnt the hard way.	You're at the top of your work life; you know what you're doing and how to achieve success.
You need to mentor someone who doesn't understand your worth. That's ok.	Your environment is supportive and improving through effort. Things are working well.
You know you have a job to do, and you know you can do it well. Get moving with it.	Abundance in all areas of life is coming soon through your concerted efforts.

3x8's=Travel plans changing. 4x8's=Your life plans are about to change for good.

The table showing the flow of energy from the one through to the ten of our journeys:

	Start	Learn	Do
One - three is where we do things on our own.	One (Ace) Have an idea. Something for yourself to do, or have for yourself. It could even be a new love. We often meet our love partner in a one year.	Two Learn how to do it. We take up a course, or apprenticeship. We often get engaged, or marry. It's a time for decisions.	Three Do. We put into practice everything we learnt before. We cement our relationships, we don't know much yet and things happen unexpectedly.
Four - six is where we work alongside other people.	Four Finish off small projects, have a peaceful or romantic interlude, then have an idea. Usually this idea involves other people.	Five (the middle) Transition and change. We are working with other people, and not on our own. This can be frustrating or fun. We can make changes together.	Six Be the leader to get things done. Time to shine as an employee (or mother, or boss.) and also a time that you may be challenged by others.
Seven - nine is where we use what we've learned. We are able to help ourselves and those around us.	Seven Complete projects. Take some time off to reconnect with friends and family. This is where we step into the creation of another idea or project.	Eight We already know how to proceed, and therefore don't need to learn. Now we can teach others. This is the time to teach other people and be the mentors. Excellent for success and travel.	Nine Do. Big projects are underway which include other people. We might feel overwhelmed with how much there is to do, but we're able to manage ourselves well now if we try.
Transition to start the cycle again.	Ten Finishing off large projects. Looking back at what you've achieved over the last ten years, and then have a new idea.		

Eight of Cups: Go with the Flow

When the Eight of Cups comes up in a reading it indicates that meditation and connection to spirit is something that should be very important to you. The Eight of Cups is the ultimate surrender and release card. It's time to meditate, become calm, and accept life the way that it is. There may be a need to surrender and release something or someone. It's time to let go. In the negative, this card may indicate that people are being escapists and avoiding reality. Hopefully this is movies, books and games, rather than drugs, alcohol and an avoidance of thinking about next steps in life. There may be a need to review what is being put into the body, the thought pattern, the television shows, the kind of books, food or drink or other substance aren't working in your favor. This is the fluids within the body card also, and can indicate medicines of all kinds. If this card comes up with The Hierophant then it indicates prescriptions and possible hospital given medications. If the Temperance card is also showing then it's a strong warning to ensure the medicines in the body are corrected and in balance.

Eight of Staves: Quick Changes

When the Eight of Staves shows up it means that everything is moving very quickly. Life has sped up and isn't slowing down anytime soon. This card can also indicate overseas travel, especially if it shows up near the Six of Swords. Lightning fast decisions are being or need to be made, and a lot of physical activity may be required. Enjoy the build-up of energy and the speed of ideas and movement happening when this card appears. Don't stop for anything!

Eight of Swords: Inner Journeys and Healing

The Eight of Swords is the inner healing card. This can indicate that thoughts are zipping around and everyone's got different ideas on how to complete projects. This card can indicate that people want things their way and may be trying to manipulate others for better or worse. For example, a mother tries to teach a child a lesson by dropping little hints which lead to the child becoming interested in a certain type of sport. Sometimes this can backfire and cause issues, but with the right intention, this can work well. This card reminds people that we only ever react to events when there is something inside of ourselves that is responding to those events. Everything outside of us can mirror something happening within. If people are really annoyed about something, then perhaps they need to ask themselves "what am I upset about in this situation? What has it to do with me? Why did I react like this?" This card reminds us not to blame others for our reactions.

Eight of Pentacles: Be the Mentor

The Eight of Pentacles is the card of industry and also of knowledge. This card means that people know what they're doing at work and at home and that they're at the point where they can teach others. This can indicate that people have become the master at work. It doesn't matter what position they are in and may not mean that they are the boss, however they are at the point where they have enough knowledge that they can show other people how to do things. Hard won knowledge is available now. People are working together. If in the negative, this card may indicate that learning is blocked right now. People may believe they know everything when in fact there is still more learning to do.

Exercise: The Eight of Cups

Look at your Eight of Water/Cups/Heart card again and this time think of your own life. Write down ten examples where you have had the Eight of Cups energy in your life.

1) Example: when I went on a cruise. When I decided to go with the flow and not worry. When I started meditating. When I refused to look at life realistically.

_____

2)

_____

3)

_____

4)

_____

5)

_____

6)

_____

7)

_____

8)

_____

9)

_____

10)

_____

Draw your idea of what this card looks like to you.

Exercise: The Eight of Staves

Look at your Eight of Fire/Staves/Wands/Clubs and this time think of your own life. Write down ten examples where you have had the Eight of Staves energy in your life.

1) Example: when I felt like travelling overseas. When I went overseas. When I ran and ran without running out of energy.

_____

2)

_____

3)

_____

4)

_____

5)

_____

6)

_____

7)

_____

8)

_____

9)

_____

10)

_____

Draw your idea of what this card looks like to you.

Exercise: The Eight of Swords

Look at your Eight of Air/Swords/Spades card and this time think of your own life. Write down ten examples where you have had the Eight of Swords energy in your life.

1) Example: when I decided to focus internally on my own healing. When I felt manipulated by others. When I changed my mind.

_____

2)

_____

3)

_____

4)

_____

5)

_____

6)

_____

7)

_____

8)

_____

9)

_____

10)

_____

Draw your idea of what this card looks like to you.

Exercise: The Eight of Pentacles

Look at your Eight of Earth/Pentacles/Diamonds/Coins card and think of your own life. Write down ten examples where you have had the Eight of Pentacles energy in your life.

1) Example: when I was working so well in my job that I was asked to teach other people. When I decided to work with others and we did well. Opening my business.

2)

3)

4)

5)

6)

7)

8)

9)

10)

Draw your idea of what this card looks like to you.

35. Sample Question for Course

Francis wants to work on her own and build a business and one of the cards drawn in the outcome space is the Eight of Pentacles. What do you tell her?

A. The Eight of Pentacles can indicate that the sky's the limit. If you wanted to work overseas right now, you could. If you wanted to work at a fly in / fly out job, you could. When this card shows up you need a change. The time is right.

B. The Eight of Pentacles indicates that you could go anywhere and do anything right now, especially if you've been going round and round in circles trying to figure out what to do next. It's time to have a think about your future and consider making a change. Don't block yourself.

C. The Eight of Pentacles indicates a knowledge of what you are doing and can therefore indicate a successful business. Go for it.

36. Sample Question for Course

Francis draws four cards, all of them eights. What do you tell her?

A. Eights are travel cards. This could mean that you're in for a journey you weren't expecting.

B. Eights mean movement, transition and change.

C. Your soul is pulling you back onto the right path – expect travel plans to change and unusual events.

D. All of the above are correct.

The Nines

"Start a huge, foolish project, like Noah… it makes absolutely no difference what people think of you."

Rumi

Nine of Cups
Water / Hearts / 9 days

You have always been the one person that everyone can rely on to give love.	A beautiful "wound" of the heart" that occurred a long time ago is still impacting you now.
Just recently something happened that has made your heart sing! Joyfulness!	Your heart is flowing over with love and joy. So much safety in family and friends.
It's hard to expect "good things" happening to you isn't it? Expect great anyway!	There is so much love and support around you right now. You're a very lucky person.
You need to be the loving support person for others now. Do it! ☺	Wow! Stay doing what you're doing. You're on the path to happiness!

3x9's=communication/letter coming which resolves a long standing issue.
4x9's=successful completion of projects.

Nine of Staves
Fire / Clubs / 9 weeks

You are usually passionate and have learnt a lot of life lessons the hard way. Maturity.	You've learnt that you are "good enough" and you own your own power and passion.
You've just come into your power, or are feeling that you need to improve.	You are "on fire" now or under intense pressure. Own your power.
You are about to come into your full power. You may not realise it now, but it's soon.	People around you are under pressure now. Support others if it's right for you to do so.
Don't let other people make you feel bad about yourself. You know you're great!	You're coming into your power and learning that you are "good enough" for all life offers.

3x9's=communication/letter coming which resolves a long standing issue.
4x9's=successful completion of projects.

Nine of Swords
Air / Spades / 9 months

You're usually able to cope with tragedy and many different ideas or challenges at once.	Tragedy in your past is causing your head to still be spinning. It wasn't fair. Heal yourself.
You've just had a draining, mentally challenging time but it's over now.	You may be feeling anxious with too many things to think about. Relax.
You're about to have to use your brain for strategy and not worry. Write things down!	You are fine, but around you there is an agony of mixed ideas and too much stress.
Think only positive thoughts now. Taking notes will avoid a lot of worry. Take deep breaths.	You're coming to a time where there is too much thinking and lots of ideas. Keep good notes.

3x9's=communication/letter coming which resolves a long standing issue.
4x9's=successful completion of projects.

Nine of Pentacles
Earth / Diamonds / 9 years

People are drawn to you. You create a safe feeling for your friends and family. Strength.	Great abundance from your past may have been frittered away, or saved. You had windfalls.
Just recently something has happened to make you feel like you've won the lotto!	You're safe and secure and are currently winning in the game of life. Great abundance.
You're about to feel like you've won something, or there may be money coming soon.	You're environment is safe and secure and there's people around you that you love and enjoy.
Windfalls can be spent. Make sure you keep some of the abundance.	Your future is looking bright and wonderful. Keep moving forward.

3x9's=communication/letter coming which resolves a long standing issue.
4x9's=successful completion of projects.

The table showing the flow of energy from the one through to the ten of our journeys:

	Start	Learn	Do
One - three is where we do things on our own.	One (Ace) Have an idea. Something for yourself to do, or have for yourself. It could even be a new love. We often meet our love partner in a one year.	Two Learn how to do it. We take up a course, or apprenticeship. We often get engaged, or marry. It's a time for decisions.	Three Do. We put into practice everything we learnt before. We cement our relationships, we don't know much yet and things happen unexpectedly.
Four - six is where we work alongside other people.	Four Finish off small projects, have a peaceful or romantic interlude, then have an idea. Usually this idea involves other people.	Five (the middle) Transition and change. We are working with other people, and not on our own. This can be frustrating or fun. We can make changes together.	Six Be the leader to get things done. Time to shine as an employee (or mother, or boss.) and also a time that you may be challenged by others.
Seven - nine is where we use what we've learned. We are able to help ourselves and those around us.	Seven Complete projects. Take some time off to reconnect with friends and family. This is where we step into the creation of another idea or project.	Eight We already know how to proceed, and therefore don't need to learn. Now we can teach others. This is the time to teach other people and be the mentors. Excellent for success and travel.	Nine Do. Big projects are underway which include other people. We might feel overwhelmed with how much there is to do, but we're able to manage ourselves well now if we try.
Transition to start the cycle again.	Ten Finishing off large projects. Looking back at what you've achieved over the last ten years, and then have a new idea.		

Nine of Cups: Windfall of the Heart

The Nine of Cups is a windfall card and reflects a windfall of the heart. It might feel like you've won the relationship lotto! There's love aplenty, but like any windfall, you can always spend it and have it move away from you. This is a wonderful card to get in a reading, but also a warning, appreciate what's coming (or what you already have) before you lose it. The card may also mean that the heart is flowing over with joy, happiness and love. Make sure to enjoy this and try to honor the feeling and appreciate what you have in order to retain it. This may also indicate family safety and security. Windfalls can be spent, so make sure you're giving love to, and looking after the important people in your life so that you don't lose them. If the question was about career, home or something else, the answer is always the same things are good, appreciate what you have and find the joy within it.

Nine of Staves: Be in Your Power

The Nine of Staves can show up when people are feeling very powerful now, or conversely are feeling quite frightened and timid and nervous about something. The Nine of Staves can be the "I'm not good enough" card until the lessons in life are learnt. After the life lessons are learnt then this becomes the "I'm in my power" card. It's easy to understand which this is as the "I'm not good enough" person will give everyone else all of their time, energy, love, and money. This person will generally not feel good about who they are and not respect themselves, and therefore will attract people into their lives who don't treat them well. The person that does feel good enough for everything life has to offer usually has people in their life that respect them and love them as much as they respect and love themselves. Look to the other cards surrounding this card to gain a better perspective of what this card means in a particular reading.

Nine of Swords: Time to Get Organized

The Nine of Swords indicates that there may be too many things to think about. This card can show up in a reading when a lot of study is required to be done and the journey ahead for people looks mentally draining and difficult. This card reminds us that if we take good notes, and think of one thing at a time, then we'll be successful at all that we want to achieve. This card can indicate that people have negative or vindictive thoughts now and may need support and assistance to get over a difficult time. If the question is about how someone feels about you, then this card may be warning that they are not happy, and may be thinking negative things about you. The message when the Nine of Swords appears in readings is always to stay calm, and be cautious about your thought patterns now. Think only positive thoughts and remove yourself from people who create a negative reaction within you.

Nine of Pentacles: Windfall of the Wallet

The Nine of Pentacles is a windfall card related to feelings of safety and security. This card shows family security, protection, abundance and safety. When this card shows up in a reading, there may be actual money coming, or it could be that people will feel like they've won the lotto. Either way, things are great. There is warning with this card though - windfalls happen occasionally, but can then be frittered away. If there's money or love that's appeared, it needs to be looked after or it will be lost. Money windfalls can be spent quickly on things that don't give long-term benefits. This card can also indicate self-made financial windfalls - you've worked hard and the money coming in is a result of the effort you have put in. This card can also indicate bonuses. If the Nine of Pentacles is drawn in a reading over and over again, there may be new money coming: in the form of a win, inheritance, or payout of some kind.

Exercise: The Nine of Cups

Look at your Nine of Water/Cups/Heart card again and this time think of your own life. Write down ten examples where you have had the Nine of Cups energy in your life.

1) Example: when I met my husband and knew it was the most wonderful connection. When I moved to a wonderful new place and felt awesome.

_____

2)

_____

3)

_____

4)

_____

5)

_____

6)

_____

7)

_____

8)

_____

9)

_____

10)

_____

Draw your idea of what this card looks like to you.

Exercise: The Nine of Staves

Look at your Nine of Fire/Staves/Wands/Clubs and this time think of your own life. Write down ten examples where you have had the Nine of Staves energy in your life.

1) Example: when I thought I wasn't good enough to finish the project but had to just keep going. When I felt in my power, or powerless.

_____

2)

_____

3)

_____

4)

_____

5)

_____

6)

_____

7)

_____

8)

_____

9)

_____

10)

_____

Draw your idea of what this card looks like to you.

Exercise: The Nine of Swords

Look at your Nine of Air/Swords/Spades card and this time think of your own life. Write down ten examples where you have had the Nine of Swords energy in your life.

1) Example: when I thought that we could all achieve great things if we worked together. When I was thinking through ideas, but having trouble with how to move forward with them.

_____

2)

_____

3)

_____

4)

_____

5)

_____

6)

_____

7)

_____

8)

_____

9)

_____

10)

_____

Draw your idea of what this card looks like to you.

Exercise: The Nine of Pentacles

Look at your Nine of Earth/Pentacles/Diamonds/Coins card and think of your own life. Write down ten examples where you have had the Nine of Pentacles energy in your life.

1) Example: when I received money back from tax. When I had an unexpected windfall. When I was financially supported by family. When I inherited a house.

_____

2)

_____

3)

_____

4)

_____

5)

_____

6)

_____

7)

_____

8)

_____

9)

_____

10)

_____

Draw your idea of what this card looks like to you.

37. Sample Question for Course

Louise asks if she'll ever have any windfalls, and draws the Nine of Pentacles. What do you tell her?

    A. Yes, the Nine of Pentacles is the windfall card.

    B. No, nines mean completing large projects, therefore you'll have to make any money that comes into your life.

    C. It's possible, the Nine of Pentacles indicates safety, security and potential self-made windfalls.

38. Sample Question for Course

Louise doesn't understand why she feels so sad all of the time and draws the Nine of Staves out of the deck. What do you tell her?

    A. The Nine of Staves is a power card, so I don't understand why you feel sad.

    B. The Nine of Staves is a fire card, so maybe you need more exercise and passion.

    C. The Nine of Staves indicates that you haven't been feeling good enough for what life has to offer. It's a reminder that you are good enough for whatever life brings.

    D. All of the above are correct.

The Tens

"It's the job that's never started as
takes longest to finish."

J.R.R. Tolkien, The Lord of the Rings

Ten of Cups
Water / Hearts / 10 days

You are community minded and know how to have long and beautiful relationships.	Any issues from your past have been released and healed. You have a big, loving heart.
Recently you've been shown how much you're loved and others have been drawn to you.	You are now in a long and happy relationship or a fulfilling career. Long term support.
You need to be the loving person for everyone around you. Open your heart and mind.	You may not feel like it but you are very well supported and loved. Surrounded by joy!
It might be time for you to extend your heart and hand to the community. You are loved.	Long term love, peace, happiness and stability are coming to you. Good times ahead.

3x10's=a lot of responsibility; try and stay strong. 4x10's=major life path changes.

Ten of Staves
Fire / Clubs / 10 weeks

You can hold many burdens at once usually. You burn through difficult issues quickly.	You came to the end of a major life cycle some time ago. You remember this well.
You've just finished climbing a steep hill with many burdens on your back. Phew!	Things are hard, but you're almost at the end of a very long, hard road. Time to stop soon!
There's about to be a lot of effort expended by you and others around you. Keep moving!	You are fine, but around you there are people that are tired and running out of energy.
Is life really as hard as you think it is? You do have burdens, but also strength. Be tough.	You're heading towards the end of a tough journey. You are soon able to drop the burden.

3x10's=a lot of responsibility; try and stay strong. 4x10's=major life path changes.

Ten of Swords
Air / Spades / 10 months

You are able to cope with a lot of thoughts at once. Stress doesn't usually impact you.	You've had an enormously stressful time in the past. This is still impacting you now.
You've just been through something horrendously challenging mentally. It's done.	You're approaching the end of a challenging road. You're almost there. Keep going.
There's about to be a stressful situation which you need to help others through. Be strong.	Your environment or the people around you are enormously stressed right now.
You need to stop worrying before you make yourself sick. Start looking on the bright side.	There's a tough time ahead with too many thoughts to think. Keep notes to avoid confusion.

3x10's=a lot of responsibility; try and stay strong. 4x10's=major life path changes.

Ten of Pentacles
Earth / Diamonds / 10 years

You are expansive and generous in all ways and draw many people to you usually.	You learnt early in life all your lessons regarding how to ensure your future abundance. ☺
You've been improving your life recently, and this will impact you long term. Enjoy it.	You have long term health and long term wealth in all areas available to you now. Great!
Improvements or renovations are needed to be done soon. You'll have everything needed.	Your environment is rock solid or being improved. The benefits are long term.
You have an enormous capacity to build abundance but you've been blocking yourself.	Long term health, wellbeing and stability are coming to you. Good times ahead. Enjoy it.

3x10's=a lot of responsibility; try and stay strong. 4x10's=major life path changes.

The table showing the flow of energy from the one through to the ten of our journeys:

	Start	Learn	Do
One - three is where we do things on our own.	One (Ace) Have an idea. Something for yourself to do, or have for yourself. It could even be a new love. We often meet our love partner in a one year.	Two Learn how to do it. We take up a course, or apprenticeship. We often get engaged, or marry. It's a time for decisions.	Three Do. We put into practice everything we learnt before. We cement our relationships, we don't know much yet and things happen unexpectedly.
Four - six is where we work alongside other people.	Four Finish off small projects, have a peaceful or romantic interlude, then have an idea. Usually this idea involves other people.	Five (the middle) Transition and change. We are working with other people, and not on our own. This can be frustrating or fun. We can make changes together.	Six Be the leader to get things done. Time to shine as an employee (or mother, or boss.) and also a time that you may be challenged by others.
Seven - nine is where we use what we've learned. We are able to help ourselves and those around us.	Seven Complete projects. Take some time off to reconnect with friends and family. This is where we step into the creation of another idea or project.	Eight We already know how to proceed, and therefore don't need to learn. Now we can teach others. This is the time to teach other people and be the mentors. Excellent for success and travel.	Nine Do. Big projects are underway which include other people. We might feel overwhelmed with how much there is to do, but we're able to manage ourselves well now if we try.
Transition to start the cycle again.	Ten Finishing off large projects. Looking back at what you've achieved over the last ten years, and then have a new idea.		

Ten of Cups: Long Term Happiness

The Ten of Cups is about long-term relationship peace and happiness. This card indicates the feeling of expansion of love into the wider family and community with ripples of love moving out and around you creating long-term joy. This card may also mean that there is a need to become more community minded (if you're not already!) and learn how to have long and beautiful relationships with other people. Long term love, peace, happiness and stability are yours. Open your heart to the wider community and to a bigger circle of friends, but don't forget your close family and friends. Ensure your loved ones are safe and happy.

Ten of Staves: Completion of Difficult Journeys

The Ten of Staves is a card of intense effort. This is not thinking. This is action and effort. This card can mean that people are working very hard and that the end of a long journey is not far away. People may not be able to see the end of the road, and may be carrying heavy burdens, but the end is near and they can soon drop the burdens that they carry. This card can indicate a trial by fire and that efforts will be rewarded. This card shows that there is a last trial before glory. Do not shirk duties if this card is present in a reading. Get the job done even though it may be hard.

Ten of Swords: Intense Mental Effort Required

The Ten of Swords is often called the stress card as it, like the Nine of Swords, indicates that there are too many things to think about. Some people thrive on ten ideas at once, and some people don't. This card however shows that an end is in sight of a long mental challenge. People have to keep calm, think about one thing at a time, and try and relax. This card can show up if children are in the middle of exams, or if there is something stressful that needs to be carefully thought out. For instance, if there have been issues at work, and a lot of people have resigned all at one time, then the people remaining have a lot to think about and too much to do. Stress relief is required! This card can show that you are thinking way too much and you need a time out. Life's not meant to be so serious. Try and stop and do something silly or active to get out of your thoughts for a while. Keep positive, all situations change.

Ten of Pentacles: Long Term Stability and Growth

The Ten of Pentacles implies long-term abundance, health and wellbeing and financial growth and stability are all available to you. Family is safe, and will continue to be safe and secure. There may be property sales and purchases, renovations and improvements. This may mean that people are getting healthier, your home will continue to improve, and your financial situation will continue to get stronger. Perhaps a successful pregnancy has occurred. Or a new business idea has been implemented ensuring growth of a business. This is a good sign if a new investment has just been considered. If in the negative, you may need to think of your future more. Are you as healthy as you could be? Are you saving money? Have you thought about your future?

Exercise: The Ten of Cups

Look at your Ten of Water/Cups/Heart card again and this time think of your own life. If you were creating a tarot deck, would you call this suit the cups or water, or something else entirely?

What would you call it? _____

Write down ten examples where you have had the Ten of Cups energy in your life.

1) Example: when I **felt** that the relationship would last forever. When the relationship felt strong. When I opened my arms to helping community members.

_____

2)

_____

3)

_____

4)

_____

5)

_____

6)

_____

7)

_____

8)

_____

9)

_____

10)

_____

Draw your idea of what this card looks like to you.

Exercise: The Ten of Staves

Look at your Ten of Fire/Staves/Wands/Clubs and this time think of your own life. If you were creating a tarot deck, would you call this suit the staves, fire or energy suit, or something else entirely?

What would you call it? _____

Write down ten examples where you have had the Ten of Staves energy in your life.

1) Example: when I completed the full project. When I decided to finally get my health together. When I came to the end of that physically tough journey.

_____

2)

_____

3)

_____

4)

_____

5)

_____

6)

_____

7)

_____

8)

_____

9)

_____

10)

_____

Draw your idea of what this card looks like to you.

Exercise: The Ten of Swords

Look at your Ten of Air/Swords/Spades card and this time think of your own life. If you were creating a tarot deck, would you call this suit the swords or air suit, or something else entirely?

What would you call it? _____

Write down ten examples where you have had the Ten of Swords energy in your life.

1) Example: when I had so many new ideas that I felt my brain would pop! When I completely stressed out over an exam. When I felt like the world was against me.

_____

2)

_____

3)

_____

4)

_____

5)

_____

6)

_____

7)

_____

8)

_____

9)

_____

10)

_____

Draw your idea of what this card looks like to you.

Exercise: The Ten of Pentacles

Look at your Ten of Earth/Pentacles/Diamonds/Coins card and think of your own life. If you were creating a tarot deck, would you call this suit the pentacles or earth suit, or something else entirely?

What would you call it? _____

Write down ten examples where you have had the Ten of Pentacles energy in your life.

1) Example: when I completed the sale or purchase of a house. When I reaped the benefits of my garden.

_____

2)

_____

3)

_____

4)

_____

5)

_____

6)

_____

7)

_____

8)

_____

9)

_____

10)

_____

Draw your idea of what this card looks like to you.

39. Sample Question for Course

If someone asked a question around whether or not their relationship would be happy, drew one card and it was the Ten of Cups, what would you tell them?

A. You'll have long term wealth.
B. There's a lot of stress around you.
C. This card indicates long-term happiness is available to you.
D. You'll be very messy and emotional and have trouble being sensible.

40. Sample Question for Course

Ronan asks if he'll be happy and draws the Ten of Staves. What do you tell him?

A. This card indicates long-term happiness is available to you.
B. This card shows a lot of effort, so you won't be happy.
C. This card shows a trial before happiness.
D. This card asks you to put down a massive burden.

CHAPTER EIGHT

The Court Cards

We are all a balance of masculine and feminine. A strong woman can be seen as quite masculine, and men sometimes have a strong feminine side.

To me, the feminine is linked to the heart, and the masculine is linked to the mind, therefore we are a mix of both feminine and masculine and we do well when we are balanced - using both our heart and our mind. "How does it feel?" Is a heart centred question, and "what do you think?" is a mind centered question.

When we are in our feminine energy we can be loving or chaotic and emotional. People mistake the feminine energy as being a weeping, crazy mess of emotions. This is not true. The feminine energy is that energy we use when we create artwork, and enjoy a sunset without having to describe what a sunset is. The feminine is that place of surrender where we don't try and control our environment.

The feminine energy can be described as coming from the heart.

When we are in our masculine energy we are thinking, using the mind and being in control. Often people mistake being masculine as being a bully, or pushing people around. This is untrue. When we are in our masculine energy we are sensible, organized, and think and plan logically. Generally when we are in our masculine we are trying to do implement something specific with a set process. For instance: project management or accountancy might be considered masculine careers, and art and clothes design might be considered feminine careers.

The masculine energy is of the mind.

There are sixteen court cards in a tarot deck and they are neither male nor female. They are generally masculine or feminine and not necessarily a man or woman specifically.

The court cards are placed into this order: page/princess, prince, queen and king. The page is feminine, the prince is masculine, the queen is feminine, and the king is masculine. Sometimes this means: girl, boy, woman, man, but sometimes it shows the emotional characteristics of both men and women at certain stages of life. We might be the page when we are nervous about something, or starting something new, regardless of gender.

1) Feminine: Page/Princess/Jack

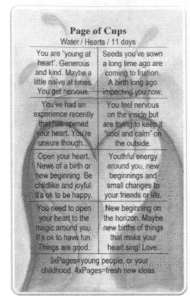

Page of Cups
Water / Hearts / 11 days

You are "young at heart". Generous and kind. Maybe a little naïve at times. You get nervous.	Seeds you've sown a long time ago are coming to fruition. A birth long ago impacting you now.
You've had an experience recently that has opened your heart. You're unsure though.	You feel nervous on the inside but are trying to keep it "cool and calm" on the outside.
Open your heart. News of a birth or new beginning. Be childlike and joyful. It's ok to be happy.	Youthful energy around you, new beginnings and small changes to your friends or life.
You need to open your heart to the magic around you. It's ok to have fun. Things are good.	New beginning on the horizon. Maybe new births of things that make your heart sing! Love.

3xPages=young people, or your childhood. 4xPages=fresh new ideas.

Page of Staves
Fire / Clubs / 11 weeks

You're good at starting new businesses, or building upon good ideas. Creator.	You've had itchy feet in your past and are feeling the energy of this again now.
You've been thinking about making changes or travelling recently.	You have "itchy feet"; is it just travel, a person, or a career change?
You need to travel or change your life. Make sensible decisions as change is needed.	You have youthful and energetic people around you that may be making a mess.
You need to look around yourself and see what the world has to offer you. Don't block your own growth.	You're heading towards some kind of travel and change. Life is not going to be boring! Passion coming.

3xPages=young people, or your childhood. 4xPages=fresh new ideas.

Page of Swords
Air / Spades / 11 months

You're usually good with coming up with new ideas and keep secrets for other people.	You made decisions in the past that you may not be proud of. Lessons learnt.
Recent secrets or events that need to be kept in the mind rather than spoken.	Right now you are the holder of secrets. Sharp intellect and ideas.
Secrets are crossing you. You may have to keep some, or others are hiding the facts.	Be cautious. There are too many secrets around you now; be careful what you say.
You need to stop telling other people everything you do as you have great ideas, but are too easily influenced.	You're heading towards some kind of new idea or plan which is best kept quiet for a little bit longer. Confidence.

3xPages=young people, or your childhood. 4xPages=fresh new ideas.

Page of Pentacles
Earth / Diamonds / 11 years

You're usually good at coming up with new ideas for your long term wealth and joy.	There's been a long journey in regard to building wealth and long term health.
You've recently been considering improving your life. Sowing the seeds for change.	Right now its little things you do that will have positive long term impacts. Consider carefully.
You're about to sow seeds for change. You need to stay grounded and be sensible.	Young energy around you. A feeling of fresh, but gentle starts which are nurturing.
It's ok to start dreaming of a better life. Dream big but move forward steadily.	You're moving into a time where you can't seem to stop improving your life. Abundance / work.

3xPages=young people, or your childhood. 4xPages=fresh new ideas.

The page is a youth and is seen as the youngest and therefore the least mature member of the tarot. In some decks this card is called the princess or the jack. As the page is feminine, drawing a page in a reading can show that someone is working from their heart and not their mind.

2) Masculine: Prince/Knight

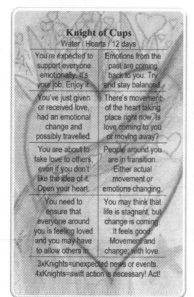

Knight of Cups
Water / Hearts / 12 days

You're expected to support everyone emotionally. It's your job. Enjoy it.	Emotions from the past are coming back to you. Try and stay balanced.
You've just given or received love, had an emotional change and possibly travelled.	There's movement of the heart taking place right now. Is love coming to you or moving away?
You are about to take love to others, even if you don't like the idea of it. Open your heart.	People around you are in transition. Either actual movement or emotions changing.
You need to ensure that everyone around you is feeling loved and you may have to allow others in.	You may think that life is stagnant, but change is coming. It feels good. Movement and change with love.

3xKnights=unexpected news or events.
4xKnights=swift action is necessary! Act!

Knight of Staves
Fire / Clubs / 12 weeks

You usually move with passion and excitement through life. You act swiftly when needed.	You wanted too, or have, changed your life quickly in the past and this is now impacting you.
You've recently had, or wanted, change. There's passion stirring.	You're on the move. Passion and energy being used for now. Caution.
You're entering a time where you have to move fast to keep up with changing events.	You're environment is changing at the moment. There's a lot of passionate energy around you.
You need to act quickly. Now is not the time for too much thinking. Do what you need too. Act swiftly now!	You're heading towards a change for the better or worse. Things are starting to speed up and get exciting.

3xKnights=unexpected news or events.
4xKnights=swift action is necessary! Act!

Knight of Swords
Air / Spades / 12 months

You usually have ideas or make changes swiftly without emotions interfering.	You've moved quickly in the past and those changes are now impacting you. Past changes.
You've recently been thinking about a change, or have done it.	Your thoughts are racing away with you. Keep your thoughts positive.
You need to come up with great ideas which bring long term change and joy. Plan then act.	Others are making plans to change their lives which may impact you. Speedy thoughts.
Charge! There's lightning fast thought needed and swift decisions to be made. Get on with it. Don't delay.	You're moving into a time where life is speeding up and heading in the directions of your dreams. Enjoy!

3xKnights=unexpected news or events
4xKnights=swift action is necessary! Act!

Knight of Pentacles
Earth / Diamonds / 12 years

You're usually good with changing where you live and what you do.	Memories of a past move or change you've made are impacting you now.
You've just had to change something; a job, an attitude, a move to a new house maybe?	You need to run to keep up with your own life now. You have opportunities coming to you.
You're about to speed up and make great changes which bring abundance.	Your environment is on the move. Things or people are changing around you.
It might be time to consider changing your career or living environment. Maybe just a clean out is required.	You're on the move; the future shows a different environment around you at work or at home.

3xKnights=unexpected news or events.
4xKnights=swift action is necessary! Act!

The knight is the young adult and is seen as the wiser and older brother (or sister) to the page, and therefore more mature, and able to learn lessons more easily than the page. As the prince is a masculine card it shows movement and a need to do something.

3) Feminine: Queen

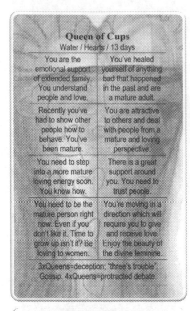

Queen of Cups
Water / Hearts / 13 days

You are the emotional support of extended family. You understand people and love.	You've healed yourself of anything bad that happened in the past and are a mature adult.
Recently you've had to show other people how to behave. You've been mature.	You are attractive to others and deal with people from a mature and loving perspective.
You need to step into a more mature loving energy soon. You know how.	There is a great support around you. You need to trust people.
You need to be the mature person right now. Even if you don't like it. Time to grow up isn't it? Be loving to women.	You're moving in a direction which will require you to give and receive love. Enjoy the beauty of the divine feminine.

3xQueens=deception; "three's trouble". Gossip. 4xQueens=protracted debate.

Queen of Staves
Fire / Clubs / 13 weeks

You are a creative person who has learnt everything the hard way and can now teach.	A birth, or learning from the past coming forward. Passionate energy. A great teacher.
Recently you've started to create, either teaching others or becoming pregnant.	You are the "fire of creation" now. The passionate teacher or pregnant, maybe just with ideas.
You're about to become a person of fire and creativity, passion or pregnancy.	Passion and knowledge are around you now. People are happy to share with you.
Don't block a wonderful and happy new life which you can create now.	You are becoming a person who can create. There's energy coming out from your body.

3xQueens=deception; "three's trouble". Gossip. 4xQueens=protracted debate.

Queen of Swords
Air / Spades / 13 Months

You are usually a strategist who is able to assist other people. Thoughtful and capable.	You've learnt that people can work together, even if they don't get along very well.
Recently you've had to be the clear minded person that supports others using foresight.	You are the master of thought and strategy on behalf of others now. Be kind to others.
You need to use clear thought processes now for the greater good of all around you.	You have a keen strategist around you. Rely on them, even though they seem uncaring.
You are an intelligent and thoughtful person. Try to expand and strategise now.	You are becoming the master of thought. Give your clarity and support to other people.

3xQueens=deception; "three's trouble". Gossip. 4xQueens=protracted debate.

Queen of Pentacles
Earth / Diamonds / 13 years

You mean support and growth for all of the people around you.	You've been the provider for a long time; food, shelter, clothing and love.
Recent impacts by the mothering energies. Very grounded and nurturing recently.	You are the giver of food, shelter, clothing and love to yourself and others around you now.
You need to move into the nurturing, grounded energy soon. Be kind and give to others.	There's great "mother" support around you; all of your needs are provided to you.
You need to open to the nurturing energy within you. Be the provider of food, shelter, clothing and love.	You're heading towards a time of abundance for yourself and an ability to give to others. Growth.

3xQueens=deception; "three's trouble". Gossip. 4xQueens=protracted debate.

The queen is an adult and is partner and equal to the king. The queen likes to work with other people and the king likes to do it his way. We often switch between being the queen and the king in our lives and this does not necessarily indicate male or female. The queen will listen to everyone around herself, and then do exactly what she believes is right, getting advice and wisdom and then doing it her way anyway. The queen is gentle, but strong. Kind but definitely not weak!

4) Masculine - King

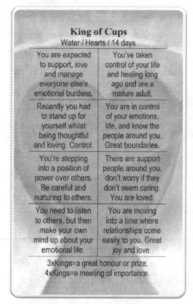

King of Cups
Water / Hearts / 14 days

You are expected to support, love and manage everyone else's emotional burdens.	You've taken control of your life and healing long ago and are a mature adult.
Recently you had to stand up for yourself whilst being thoughtful and loving. Control.	You are in control of your emotions, life, and know the people around you. Great boundaries.
You're stepping into a position of power over others. Be careful and nurturing to others.	There are support people around you, don't worry if they don't seem caring. You are loved.
You need to listen to others, but then make your own mind up about your emotional life.	You are moving into a time where relationships come easily to you. Great joy and love.

3xKings=a great honour or prize.
4xKings=a meeting of importance.

King of Staves
Fire / Clubs / 14 weeks

You are a strong person who has learnt everything the hard way. The worldly teacher.	You've learnt a lot but may not be completely proud of your past. Hard-won wisdom.
Recently you've come into your power. You know what you want and how to get it.	You're a controlled energy of fire and power now. You're ready to teach or give passion.
You need to be kind, strong and passionate now. Show others how fabulous you are.	You are surrounded by knowledge, learning, creativity and passion.
If you have a burning desire to do something with your life, it's time to learn how. Learn.	You are becoming the "master of your realm". You are learning and becoming wise.

3xKings=a great honour or prize.
4xKings=a meeting of importance.

King of Swords
Air / Spades / 14 months

You are a strong intellectual who can impart wisdom to others who are confused by life.	You've learnt how to be an adult using intellect. You usually "think", not "feel". Old plans.
Recently you've had to be the person that leads others using clarity of thinking.	You are the master of thought and strategy and need to be the leader for others now.
You need to listen to others, and then strategise your own life. Make plans which benefit all.	There's someone very smart around you. They are diligent and clever; a strategist.
You are an intelligent and in control person. It's time for you to plan your future.	You are becoming the master of thought. You'll be the leader for others. Be caring.

3xKings=a great honour or prize.
4xKings=a meeting of importance.

King of Pentacles
Earth / Diamonds / 14 years

You are grounding to everyone around you. You are the master of stability and abundance.	You learnt a long time ago to be strong, sensible, and reliable. You are a provider.
Recent impacts by your father or you have become more grounded and realistic recently.	You are the provider of food, shelter, clothing and love to yourself and others now.
You need to move into the controlled, grounded energy now. It's time to be sensible and calm.	Your environment is grounding and protective and everything is provided to you.
You need to open to the grounded energy within you. Be the provider of shelter and safety.	You're becoming the master of abundance and growth. Enjoy the expansion coming.

3xKings=a great honour or prize.
4xKings=a meeting of importance.

The king is an adult and is partner and equal to the queen. The King likes to do everything his way whereas the queen tries to work with other people. We often switch between being the king and the queen as we go about our lives and this does not necessarily indicate male or female. The King will listen to everyone around himself, if he so chooses to, but then can easily disregard advice and will charge ahead in the direction that he feels is right.

41. Sample Question for Course

Jenny wants to know if she is pregnant with a boy or a girl, what do you tell her when she draws the Page of Swords?

A. It's a surprise.
B. The feminine is indicated – the child is likely to be a girl, however it could be a gentle-hearted boy.
C. The child is a girl.
D. None of the above.

42. Sample Question for Course

Natasha wants to know how to handle a situation at work and draws the King of Swords. What do you tell her?

A. Be ruthless – say what you want.
B. Quit immediately and move onto something better.
C. The king is usually the boss, so it's surprising that you have a hard situation at work. It's necessary to show leadership and courage right now.
D. The king listens to others, but then makes decisions on his own – you need to talk through the issues using little emotions, and mostly logic as swords is the air suit and the king is the masculine – or mind processes.

The Page

Feminine: Page/Princess/Jack

The page is a youth and is seen as the youngest of the court cards, and therefore the least mature member of the tarot. In some decks this card is called the princess or the jack. As the page is feminine, drawing a page can show that someone is working from their heart and not their mind.

Page	The Knight	The Queen	The King
The child, the immature. Feelings of uncertainty and new beginnings. The first steps to a new world, and a new life.	The teenager. All about the changing nature of life, wanting to move out, move on, improve, progress and grow up.	The mother. The provider of advice, food, shelter, clothing, love and the passionate creator of life.	The father. Master of advice, food, shelter, clothing, love and the passionate creator of life.

Page of Cups: The Emotional Child

The Page of Cups is someone that has a lot of turbulent emotions on the inside, yet can sometimes maintain a cool and calm outward appearance. This page of water may become emotional and not know what to do with the turbulent emotions they are feeling. This card may also indicate a young person or young people, news of a birth or new beginning, or it might simply be asking that you start slowly in a new endeavor or relationship. This card reflects a need for calm.

Page of Staves: The Passionate Child

The Page of Staves reflects itchy feet, a need to become more active, be more daring, travel or start exercising. This page of fire may burn themselves on the flame of their passions. There's no point telling the Page of Staves that they're doing anything risky as they want to learn everything the hard way. This card may simply show that you are becoming fitter and more passionate about life. To me, the Page of Staves is a traveller and a messenger, as they are doing something, and not just sitting about waiting for something to come to them. This is the get motivated and get moving card.

Page of Swords: The Witty Child

The Page of Swords is seen as a thinker. A charismatic and youthful person who can attract others through the wittiness and cleverness of their thinking. This person may seem youthful and full of charisma but this page of air may cut themselves on their brilliant, yet flawed, ideas. The Page of Swords has an interesting life, and it can get even more interesting if they get caught out doing something they shouldn't be. This card may be a reminder to seek wise counsel (and not just any advice) before putting plans into motion, as you may not have thought through all of the details. Interestingly, the Page of Swords makes an excellent teacher of adults and can sometimes indicate going back to school at a later age. Often the education we receive at the hands of the Page of Swords cuts deep.

Page of Pentacles: The Practical Child

The Page of Pentacles implies growth. This page of earth may not know how to start their growth cycle and may take a little bit of time to really get moving. The seed of new abundance is being planted and there is hope that new endeavors of all kinds will be coming into your future, through your careful nurturing of new ideas and plans. This card may remind us to start at the beginning. Promote steady growth rather than trying to build too quickly too soon. Plant the seeds for change and allow time to assist you. Nurture yourself now so that you can support others later. The Page of Pentacles may show up when you're considering a long term venture of any kind, including bringing a child into the family. The main message behind this page, is an emphasis on starting fresh and growing slowly, ensuring that the step by step process is sound and stable. This is a take things slow and steady card.

Exercise: The Page of Cups

Look at your Page of Water/Cups/Heart card again and this time think of your own life. Write down ten examples where you have had the Page of Cups energy in your life.

1) Example: news of a birth. When I was a young child. When I felt really sad but didn't know how to say it, and made a mess of relationships.

_____

2)

_____

3)

_____

4)

_____

5)

_____

6)

_____

7)

_____

8)

_____

9)

_____

10)

_____

Draw your idea of what this card looks like to you.

Exercise: The Page of Staves

Look at your Page of Fire/Staves/Wands/Clubs and this time think of your own life. Write down ten examples where you have had the Page of Staves energy in your life.

1) Example: when I decided that I was going to travel. When I contacted an old friend and had a big chat.

_____

2)

_____

3)

_____

4)

_____

5)

_____

6)

_____

7)

_____

8)

_____

9)

_____

10)

_____

Draw your idea of what this card looks like to you.

Exercise: The Page of Swords

Look at your Page of Air/Swords/Spades card and this time think of your own life. Write down ten examples where you have had the Page of Swords energy in your life.

1) Example: when I led by example. When I helped out a work colleague with something they couldn't understand. When I stole my husband's last chocolate.

2)

3)

4)

5)

6)

7)

8)

9)

10)

Draw your idea of what this card looks like to you.

Exercise: The Page of Pentacles

Look at your Page of Earth/Pentacles/Diamonds/Coins card and think of your own life. Write down ten examples where you have had the Page of Pentacles energy in your life.

1) Example: when I started to put money into the bank. When I decided to learn more about financial matters. When I decided to plant a vegetable garden.

2)

3)

4)

5)

6)

7)

8)

9)

10)

Draw your idea of what this card looks like to you.

43. Sample Question for Course

Jane asks a question about a friend of hers and draws the Page of Swords card. What do you tell her?

A. The Page of Swords can mean that people aren't being honest.
B. This card shows stress and worry.
C. This card indicates someone who is clever and witty, someone who holds many secrets.
D. This card reflects her desire to travel and experience life.

44. Sample Question for Course

Jane wants to know how long it will be before she buys a house, and draws the Page of Pentacles. What do you tell her?

A. The Page of Pentacles means eleven years, however it might not be an answer to the timeframe question, it may just mean that it will take time to build wealth.
B. This card indicates that small seeds grow over time – therefore no timeframe is indicated.
C. Both the above are correct.

The Knight

Masculine: Prince, Knight

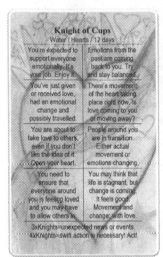

The knight is the young adult and is seen as the wiser and older brother (or sister) to the page, and therefore more mature, and able to learn lessons more easily than the page. As the knight is masculine, drawing a knight can show that someone is working from their mind and not their heart.

Page	The Knight	The Queen	The King
The child, the immature. Feelings of uncertainty and new beginnings. The first steps to a new world, and a new life.	The teenager. All about the changing nature of life, wanting to move out, move on, improve, progress and grow up.	The mother. The provider of advice, food, shelter, clothing, love and the passionate creator of life.	The father. Master of advice, food, shelter, clothing, love and the passionate creator of life.

Knight of Cups: Emotional Changes

The Knight of Cups shows movement of emotions. There could be love moving towards you, or love could be moving away from you. It's also possible that you are the one that needs to take love to someone, or take it away from someone. It's best to read the other cards to see what is really required. This knight of water wants to change their emotional life and may need to keep their hearts open and move through emotional issues rather than try and ignore them. This knight may be ready to change the direction of their affections without much notice. This person may think that they know everything, and in some cases, this can indicate that they really do know everything that they need to know for now. Life's changing and the knight is on his noble steed and ready to go. This card reminds us to try and keep an open heart, as blockages in the heart can cause heart pain.

Knight of Staves: Action and Adventure

The Knight of Staves indicates that swift action is required. This knight of fire wants to move and will burn through any issue quickly. If this is about their work or travel, then away they go! Life's changing and the knight is ready for adventure. This person might be very sporty and able to take their sporting achievements across boundaries: for instance, overseas. This person may even like to work overseas. At the very least, this person will want to cross boundaries for instance, travel to another state.

Knight of Swords: Plans for Change

The Knight of Swords implies fast thinking, clear thought and a need to make plans to change your life. Planning, not necessarily doing. As this is an air sign, the Knight wants to change their life, but needs to think about it before leaping into change. This knight may make changes without too much thought and then regret it later, planning before creating change, may be the lesson this person needs to learn. Life's changing and the knight is on his noble steed and ready for movement! You may want to change things about your life, or things might be changing so fast you can't think straight! Either way, there will be a move happen within the next twelve months.

Knight of Pentacles: Changes at Home or Work

The Knight of Pentacles implies that your environment is on the move. This knight of earth wants change and will be steady and practical about it. If this is about work or travel, then they want to move, but will try and plan everything first. Life's changing and the knight is on his noble steed and ready for movement! This may be a mature teenager who is ready to move out. The teenager thinks that they know everything, and in some cases, this can indicate that they really do know everything that they need to know for now. This card indicates right timing to change jobs, home, or renovate and improve your living environment. This card can also remind us to become more energetic, to consider moving, or improving or changing our work or home life. You may not know where to start, but start anyway!

Exercise: The Knight of Cups

Look at your Knight of Water/Cups/Heart card again and this time think of your own life
Write down ten examples where you have had the Knight of Cups energy in your life.

1) Example: when I opened my heart back up to my brother. When I chose to travel to
see family.

_____

2)

_____

3)

_____

4)

_____

5)

_____

6)

_____

7)

_____

8)

_____

9)

_____

10)

_____

Draw your idea of what this card looks like to you.

Exercise: The Knight of Staves

Look at your Knight of Fire/Staves/Wands/Clubs and this time think of your own life. Write down ten examples where you have had the Knight of Staves energy in your life.

1) Example: when I travelled. When I won the sports carnival. When I went dancing.

_____

2)

_____

3)

_____

4)

_____

5)

_____

6)

_____

7)

_____

8)

_____

9)

_____

10)

_____

Draw your idea of what this card looks like to you.

Exercise: The Knight of Swords

Look at your Knight of Air/Swords/Spades card and this time think of your own life. Write down ten examples where you have had the Knight of Swords energy in your life.

1) Example: when I made plans to change my life. When I decided that the family would move within the next year.

2)

3)

4)

5)

6)

7)

8)

9)

10)

Draw your idea of what this card looks like to you.

Exercise - The Knight of Pentacles

Look at your Knight of Earth/Pentacles/Diamonds/Coins card and think of your own life. Write down ten examples where you have had the Knight of Pentacles energy in your life.

1) Example: when I changed jobs. When I renovated my home. When I kept saving money.

_____

2)

_____

3)

_____

4)

_____

5)

_____

6)

_____

7)

_____

8)

_____

9)

_____

10)

_____

Draw your idea of what this card looks like to you.

45. Sample Question for Course

The Knight of Pentacles is drawn in a reading and placed in the environment space. What do you tell the person?

    A. Knights mean movement, and this is movement of food, shelter and clothing. Maybe you're moving home, or moving job which impacts your ability to provide.

    B. This card means continuing stability.

    C. People are coming and going. It's going to be busy.

    D. Someone is coming soon to give you money.

46. Sample Question for Course

Three knights are showing in a reading. What do you say?

    A. Knights mean movement, I'd suggest you make changes right now.

    B. Knights mean movement - someone around you is going to move.

    C. Three knights cancel each other out – there's a period of stagnation now.

    D. Consider what is happening in your life and make sure you're planning ahead as three knights mean sudden movement, or a lot happening and changing now.

The Queen

Feminine: Queen

The queen is an adult and is partner and equal to the king. The queen likes to work with other people and the king likes to do things way. We often switch between being the queen and the king in our lives and this does not necessarily indicate male or female, as previously discussed.

The queen will listen to everyone around herself, and then do exactly what she believes is right, getting advice and guidance from others, and then doing things her way anyway. The queen is gentle, but strong. Kind but definitely not weak!

The queen is the mother card of the deck, however the Queen of Cups and the Queen of Pentacles is more likely to be a traditional at home with the children type of mother, and the Queen of Staves and Queen of Swords is more likely to want to rule over others in business.

Page	The Knight	The Queen	The King
The child, the immature. Feelings of uncertainty and new beginnings. The first steps to a new world, and a new life.	The teenager. All about the changing nature of life, wanting to move out, move on, improve, progress and grow up.	The mother. The provider of advice, food, shelter, clothing, love and the passionate creator of life.	The father. Master of advice, food, shelter, clothing, love and the passionate creator of life.

Queen of Cups: Mother of Love

The Queen of Cups can indicate a person of beauty, harmony, compassion and understanding. The queen of water (emotions) has learnt how to have successful relationships with many different types of people and is the gentlest queen in the tarot. The Queen of Cups is someone that likes to give love to people. The Queen of Cups may be asking you to become a more caring and loving person in any kind of situation. The Queen of Cups is a person who has learnt life's lessons regarding relationships and is ready to give and receive love (like the King.) This is a person that can easily work with other people and understands the rules of relating to others from the heart. This queen needs to ensure she doesn't become the martyr and put others before herself.

Queen of Staves: Mother of Passion

The Queen of Staves can indicate a person of passion and education, a teacher, and it can also indicate pregnancy. The queen of fire has learnt a lot of life lessons by walking through the fire, making mistakes as a young adult and becoming wise through lessons learnt the hard way rather than listening to, and following, other people's advice. The Queen of Staves is asking that you become a wise and mature person who is able to handle a lot of passion without causing harm to others. The Queen of Staves has a lot of herself to give and is often a teacher.

Queen of Swords: Mother of Ideas

The Queen of Swords can indicate a strategist and a planner, and is one of the more thinking and less emotional and feeling people within the Tarot. Even though the queen is a feminine sign, this is a woman of balance and purpose. The head does go before the heart with this lady, but she'll organize things to help others, so her intention are good; think of the female surgeon, she's wanting to help, but will cut you open to do it. The queen of air has learnt a lot of life lessons through deep thought and by thinking things through to the logical conclusions. This queen may have learnt a lot of life lessons from reviewing the mistakes that other people have made and choosing a different life path for themselves. The Queen of Swords is asking that you become a strategist and a planner and try not to let undue emotions interfere with organizing your life for the greater good of yourself, and for those people around you.

Queen of Pentacles: Mother of Abundance

The Queen of Pentacles is a person who has enough food, shelter, clothing and love to give to others, therefore this card can be seen as the mother of children. The Queen of Pentacles is able to provide and nurture many people. The Queen of Pentacles is a person who has learnt life's lessons regarding abundance matters, and if you have not yet learnt this lesson, the queen may have shown up in your reading to remind you to take care of the fundamentals in life; food, shelter, clothing and most of all love. The Queen of Pentacles is the master of home and money, and therefore could very well have a home based business.

Exercise: The Queen of Cups

Look at your Queen of Water/Cups/Heart card again and this time think of your own life. Write down ten examples where you have had the Queen of Cups energy in your life.

1) Example: the love that overflowed from my heart when I became a parent. When I managed a team of people.

2)

3)

4)

5)

6)

7)

8)

9)

10)

Draw your idea of what this card looks like to you.

Exercise: Queen of Staves

Look at your Queen of Fire/Staves/Wands/Clubs and this time think of your own life. Write down ten examples where you have had the Queen of Staves energy in your life.

1) Example: when I had travelled a while. When I opened up a clothing shop. When I started teaching art.

_____

2)

_____

3)

_____

4)

_____

5)

_____

6)

_____

7)

_____

8)

_____

9)

_____

10)

_____

Draw your idea of what this card looks like to you.

Exercise: The Queen of Swords

Look at your Queen of Air/Swords/Spades card and this time think of your own life. Write down ten examples where you have had the Queen of Swords energy in your life.

1) Example: when I went to the accountant. When I assisted in developing a business plan.

_____

2)

_____

3)

_____

4)

_____

5)

_____

6)

_____

7)

_____

8)

_____

9)

_____

10)

_____

Draw your idea of what this card looks like to you.

Exercise: Queen of Pentacles

Look at your Queen of Earth/Pentacles/Diamonds/Coins card and think of your own life. Write down ten examples where you have had the Queen of Pentacles energy in your life.

1) Example: when I started a home based business. When I organized my children and family.

_____

2)

_____

3)

_____

4)

_____

5)

_____

6)

_____

7)

_____

8)

_____

9)

_____

10)

_____

Draw your idea of what this card looks like to you.

47. Sample Question for Course

Work has been difficult for Henry and he wants to change his career. He draws out the Queen of Pentacles. Which of the below is most right?

    A. You'll have long term wealth.
    B. You may consider working from home, or managing your own business.
    C. Female friends around you can help you.

48. Sample Question for Course

Karen feels unhappy with the people around herself and asks what she needs to do to help relationships. The Queen of Cups is drawn. What do you tell her?

    A. This card asks you to be loving and wise.
    B. This card asks you to leave people behind you.
    C. This card asks you to feel sorry for others.
    D. This card suggests that other people are jealous of you.

The King

Masculine: King

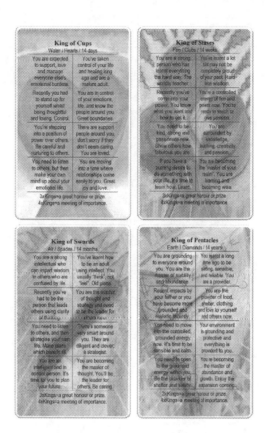

The king is an adult and is partner and equal to the queen. The king likes to do everything his way whereas the queen tries to work with other people. We often switch between being the king and the queen energy as we go about our lives and this does not necessarily indicate male or female. The King will listen to everyone around himself, if he so chooses to, but then can easily disregard advice and will charge ahead in the direction that he feels is right to do so!

The king is the father card of the deck, however the King of Cups and the King of Pentacles is more likely to be a stay-at-home dad, and the King of Staves and King of Swords is more likely to want to rule over others with a specialist skill or in business.

Generally, the king is a master of the element and can be a man or a woman.

Page	The Knight	The Queen	The King
The child, the immature. Feelings of uncertainty and new beginnings. The first steps to a new world, and a new life.	The teenager. All about the changing nature of life, wanting to move out, move on, improve, progress and grow up.	The mother. The provider of advice, food, shelter, clothing, love and the passionate creator of life.	The father. Master of advice, food, shelter, clothing, love and the passionate creator of life.

King of Cups - Master of Love

The King of Cups can indicate a person that loves many people, someone that appreciates beauty and sometimes needs to be in the spotlight. The King of Cups is a person who has learnt life's lessons regarding relationships and is ready to give and receive love (like the queen.) This is a person that can easily work with other people and understands the rules of relating to others from the heart. The king tries to listen to others, but enjoys taking control of situations, generally believing that he's doing the best thing for everyone. The King of Cups may be reminding you that it's your time to shine and allow other people to admire you!

King of Staves: Master of Passion

The King of Staves can indicate a person of passion and education, a master of their chosen trade. The king of fire has learnt a lot of life lessons by walking through the fire, making mistakes as a young adult and becoming wise through lessons learnt the hard way, rather than listening to, and following, other people's advice. The King of Staves is asking that you become a wise and mature person who is able to handle a lot of passion without causing harm to others. The King of Staves has conquered many challenges and come out as the victor! The King of Staves showing up in your reading might be reminding you how passionate and energetic you actually are and giving you a prompt to get active. This card can also be a reminder that you need to study a trade and become a specialist in your chosen.

King of Swords: Master of Thought

The King of Swords is one of the more thinking and less emotional and feeling people within the tarot. This king is a strong thinker and can see far into the future. Accounting and law are the types of fields that would attract these people. The King of Swords cannot allow emotions to interfere with the facts and always have one eye on the future. The king of air has learnt a lot of life lessons through deep thought and by thinking things through to the logical conclusions. This king may have learnt a lot of life lessons from reviewing the mistakes that other people have made and choosing a different life path for themselves. The King of Swords is asking that you become a strategist and a planner and try not to let undue emotions interfere with organizing your life for the greater good of yourself, and for those people around you. The king commands you to plan, and change, your life without becoming too emotional.

King of Pentacles: Master of Abundance

The King of Pentacles is a person who has learnt life's lessons regarding abundance matters and is generally in control of their own wealth. The King of Pentacles is a person who has enough food, shelter, clothing and love to give to others and therefore this card can be seen as the father. The King is able to provide and nurture many people, but is seen as giving tough love more so than the Queen. The King of Pentacles may be reminding you to be more controlled in dealing with others, and possibly less emotional. You may also be reminded to be the father figure for others, a warm and loving person who tries to seek understanding. The King of Pentacles can be stubborn, and if this resonates, then try and not bully others into your way of thinking. The King of Pentacles is the master of home and money, and therefore could very well have a home based business, or run a family owned company.

Exercise: The King of Cups

Look at your King of Water/Cups/Heart card again and this time think of your own life. Write down ten examples where you have had the King of Cups energy in your life.

1) Example: when I became a father. The father figure. A man who can give a wise and mature love to others. A meaningful relationship with others.

_____

2)

_____

3)

_____

4)

_____

5)

_____

6)

_____

7)

_____

8)

_____

9)

_____

10)

_____

Draw your idea of what this card looks like to you.

Exercise: The King of Staves

Look at your King of Fire/Staves/Wands/Clubs and this time think of your own life. Write down ten examples where you have had the King of Staves energy in your life.

1) Example: when I became qualified. When I finished learning everything the hard way and tried to start teaching others how to not make mistakes. When I became knowledgeable about the many countries I had visited.

_____

2)

_____

3)

_____

4)

_____

5)

_____

6)

_____

7)

_____

8)

_____

9)

_____

10)

_____

Draw your idea of what this card looks like to you.

Exercise: King of Swords

Look at your King of Air/Swords/Spades card and this time think of your own life. Write down ten examples where you have had the King of Swords energy in your life.

1) Example: when I assisted in the creation and running of a business plan through to completion. When I organized my ten year plan.

_____

2)

_____

3)

_____

4)

_____

5)

_____

6)

_____

7)

_____

8)

_____

9)

_____

10)

_____

Draw your idea of what this card looks like to you.

Exercise: King of Pentacles

Look at your King of Earth/Pentacles/Diamonds/Coins card and think of your own life. Write down ten examples where you have had the King of Pentacles energy in your life.

1) Example: when I ran a successful home based business. When I organized my children and family. When I was the voice of reason when people wanted to waste money.

_____

2)

_____

3)

_____

4)

_____

5)

_____

6)

_____

7)

_____

8)

_____

9)

_____

10)

_____

Draw your idea of what this card looks like to you.

49. Sample Question for Course

Ken wants to know if he'll ever have a family and draws three kings. What do you tell him?

A. Your fate is being decided by a higher power.
B. There are major decisions to be made which influence your future.
C. This card shows sensible people around you and mature relationships.
D. All of the above.

50. Sample Question for Course

Ken wants to know if he'll ever have a family and draws the King of Cups. What do you tell him?

A. Your fate is being decided by a higher power.
B. This is the card of loving relationships, it certainly looks like you will have one.
C. It's unlikely as the king likes to do things his own way and pushes other people aside.
D. None of the above.

CHAPTER NINE

The Major Arcana Soul Journey cards

In the numbers cards the ace (or the one) is obviously the beginning of a journey and the ten is the end. Likewise with the Major Arcana, or spirit, or soul growth cards, there is a logical beginning card: 0-The Fool card, and a logical end card: 21-The World.

There are twenty-two cards in the Major Arcana and this does confuse a lot of people as the last card is the twenty-one (21) card. I have purchased a lot of Tarot decks only to be disappointed that people have made a mistake and put a twenty-two (22) against The World card instead of a twenty-one (21.) If The World card was the twenty-second card, then The Fool should have started at one. The Fool starts at zero, therefore the twenty-second card is actually the card entitled twenty-one (21).

One is the number of beginnings usually, but in the case of the Major Arcana, the beginning card is number zero. This card is The Fool card and we have already created this card at the beginning of the book.

The journey of the soul on the earth has always been depicted within the Major Arcana starting with The Fool card representing our birth and the soul coming down into the physical body, and ending with The World card where we finish a major soul journey.

Therefore The Fool card can describe the very process of deciding to start as a baby here on the planet.

If we arrange all the cards in three rows we get the below:

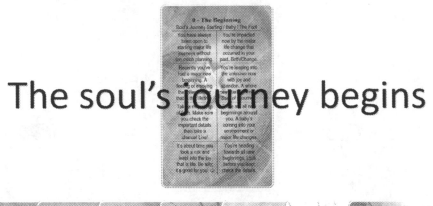

The soul's journey begins

Physical journey on Earth

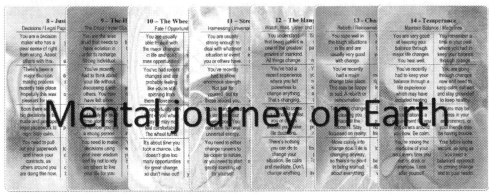

Mental journey on Earth

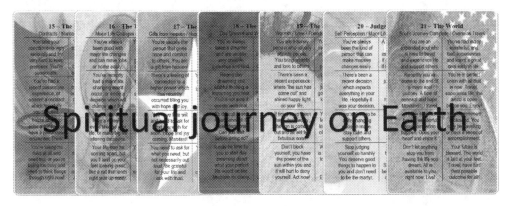

Spiritual journey on Earth

Now we are going to create our next cards.

The Physical Journey

The soul coming down unto the earth is considered The Fool card. The Fool card also describes the beginning of every major journey that the soul can take. It can describe a new career move, a new house, a new relationship, or any other new event that can impact the happiness or enlightenment of the soul.

Read through this example:

- **New Idea: "Let's build a house!"** 0 – **The Fool.** Consider this, we decide to build a house; The Fool – we embark on a whole new adventure. We've gone into this card in depth at the beginning of this book.

- **Creation: "What should it look like, be like?"** 1 – **The Magician.** Then we put our idea into action. We have to do the research, find the land, consider what we need, check and re-check details to create the space. Or we can just find a block of land and buy it without checking important details. Either way we've created something. The trouble with creating something, is we could create something that's rubbish, or we could create something that's wonderful. That's why the Magician is often associated with smoke and mirrors, those things which aren't real. When we create something, we always have a choice at how well we do it and how much effort we put into making it right.

- **Certification and Intuition: "What do we need to learn?"** 2 – **The High Priestess** is often associated with using our instincts and also with gaining certification. We might need to find out about building plans, or do a building course. We may need to learn more about what we want to do in order to then go back to the creation phase of our home project.

- **Feminine: "How I want to feel in our new home."** 3 – **The Empress** is associated with how things make us feel. You might feel bad or good, happy or sad, excited or troubled. The feminine and the masculine energy is like saying the heart and the head. We need both the masculine (it's a good idea) and the feminine (I love the colors and artwork) in order to feel that something we create is perfect. The feminine is often the creative energy that builds upon our ideas. Therefore we may say, "Well I want the walls to be cream, and the lounge room to feel inviting and cool." This isn't a sensible (of the mind) thing to say about a home before you've built it, but it gives the basis of what comes next.

- **Masculine. "I need to think this through."** 4 – **The Emperor.** We've decided that we want to build a house, we've started thinking about what certification we need, know what we want it to feel like, now we have to think practically about it. How do you build a home that feels inviting and cool in the lounge room? The logical step might be having a lounge room that's out of the path of the sun. That would ensure it stays cool all year around. The masculine, or the thinking process, may require you to write down checklists. As you move through the process of identifying logical issues with the home, you then revisit the feminine/feeling space to see how those ideas feel to you. We flip between the left and right parts of the brain all the time. The right side could be considered masculine and the left side could be considered feminine. The right side is also about logical reasoning and the left side is all about creativity and feeling.

- **Tradition. "I will need to check my plans with a governing body to seek approvals."** 5 – **The Hierophant.** We need to fit into the larger society when it comes to building a home and generally house plans need approvals from government bodies. There are rules, we can't just build our home in a school playground just because the space is there. We need to purchase a block of land from a higher authority. Once we've purchased the land, the way we lay electricity cables, plumbing cables, sewer systems, and the way that we build our home, can all be constrained by legislation and rules. It's often best to try and figure out what these are before we start planning a home, but generally there's so many rules and regulations, that it's best to make a plan, and then see if it passes rather than spend years learning the laws before even starting to plan your home. A higher authority is also God energy (whichever God you have found on your earth journey.) You might pray quite a bit whilst in the middle of building your own house, as it can be quite stressful.

- **Soul mate relationships. "Wow, working with you and the government is really testing my patience!"** 6 – **The Lovers.** We live in a world where we generally have to fit in with other people in some way. Even if we're building the house by ourselves with no other help, we still need to work with the regulating bodies to ensure that our home plans will get along with the current expectations. Soul mate relationships can take many different forms and we often don't have children with soul mates, as we generally learn our lessons and move on. Sometimes we decide to come back into a lifetime with someone because we need to learn to love them, and those relationships can be magical and beautiful and include marriage and children, the whole happily ever after scenario. Generally though, soul mate relationships are hard work.

- **Choices and successful endeavors. "Well, we've done it! House completed! Let's celebrate!"** 7 – **The Chariot.** We have many forks in the road when building a home. We make many choices. We learn to work together (soul mate relationships,) we gain approvals as we go (The Hierophant,) and we continuously check in with how we feel and what we think about our home as it develops. Do we really want that cream color? How about we go for a blue wall? That would **feel** better, and I was **thinking** that we could save money on paint by going with one color throughout, but if it would make you **feel** better, then we'll spend the money. We've come through all the lessons and we've successfully completed our home! Yay!

Now as you can see from the above example of the building of a home, the soul cards aren't in chronological order. We can have an idea and decide to change something significant (The Fool) when we're half way through building the home. We may **not** get approval (5 The Hierophant) and have to change our plan (4 The Emperor.) It may look like we're going backwards, but we've learnt something valuable (2 The High Priestess) which will help us get the whole project finished (7 The Chariot.)

1. The Magician: Creation

1 - The Magician
The Manifestation of Your Life

You are able to manifest what you think about; you have an idea and make it happen.	You've learnt how to create your life; hopefully it has substance and not just a nice façade.
Recently you've had to envision how you want your life to be. Magic may have just happened. Wow.	You're currently creating a new life for yourself. Make sure it's strong and fulfilling and not empty of meaning.
You're about to start visualising a new life for yourself or others. You may not want to do this, but you can do it.	"All that glitters isn't gold". Is your environment only looking good, or is it really good? Be careful but happy.
You need to believe in magic again. You are clever enough to create a new life.	You're going to be magic soon. Make sure it's real and grounded, and not empty prettiness.

When The Magician comes up in a reading, you are reminded that you are magical and that if you have an idea, then you can create it on the earth plane. You are the person manifesting your life.

Then we put our idea into action. We have to do the research, find the land, consider what we need, check and re-check details to create the space. Or we can just find a block of land and buy it without checking important details. Either way we've created something. The trouble with creating something, is we could create something that's rubbish, or we could create something that's wonderful. That's why magicians are often associated with smoke and mirrors - those things that aren't real. When we create something, we always have a choice at how well we do it and how much effort we put into making it right.

Some examples of what this card may mean when it comes up in a reading are below:

- A need to create a better life for yourself.
- That you are able to do more than you think you can, in order to change your current circumstances.

- That you need to be careful what you think about, as your thoughts are creating your future.
- To create a life of substance. Not just a life that looks good from the outside.
- That you can trick people, mesmerize people, and pretend you are someone that you are not.

If this comes up about someone you have asked about, they could actually be quite lucky and magical, or they could just be an illusion, with the reality hidden below.

This card may show up after a new beginning, and before all of the details have been sorted through. It indicates that you can have your life the way you want it in this case.

Exercise: The Magician

Look at The Magician card again and this time think of your own life.
If you were creating a tarot deck, would you call this suit the spirit suit, or Major Arcana, or something else entirely?
What would you call it? _____
Write down ten examples where you have had The Magician energy in your life. Don't focus on trying to be right, just go with what **feels** right for you. Go back to the previous chapter and re-read that if you need too.

1) Example: when I decided what color to paint a room. When I decided that I could have my relationship anyway I chose too.

_____

2)

_____

3)

_____

4)

_____

5)

_____

6)

_____

7)

_____

8)

_____

9)

_____

10)

_____

Draw your idea of what this card looks like to you.

2. The High Priestess: Certification and Intuition

2 - The High Priestess
The First Teacher / Study / Intuition

You are a very wise and intuitive person who is connected to spirit. Share knowledge.	You've learnt that you need to follow your instincts, or you've achieved certification.
Recently you've been in tune with how the universe works or you've just achieved something great!	You need to listen to your inner guidance right now. It's very accurate. Feminine intuition or divine guidance.
You're either becoming very in tune with spiritual guidance, or you're about to achieve certification.	You have someone around you who is amazingly intuitive or you have an excellent learning opportunity now.
You need to start following your own inner guidance rather than relying on other people.	You're becoming a "wise one". People will require you in the future for your in tune guidance.

The High Priestess is the first teacher in the soul's journey. The first teacher is usually instinct therefore this can indicate that the person is very intuitive and that divine guidance is available to the person being read for.

Some examples of what this card may mean when it comes up in a reading are below:

- Certification.
- Success at courses and study.
- A need to open to divine guidance and meditate more; to become more spiritual and open to listening to the divine energies.
- That there is a need to learn and listen to others.
- That the person needs to open up their ability to listen to guidance, and maybe use this more for a career. (Tarot card reader, Reiki worker, Massage therapist or energy worker of any kind.)

For instance, this card may show up if the person has a natural ability to listen to divine guidance. It may also appear if someone is nervous about undertaking a new beginning in life; the message is everything will be available when you need it, especially knowledge.

Exercise: The High Priestess

Look at The High Priestess card again and this time think of your own life. Write down ten examples where you have had The High Priestess energy in your life.

1) Example: when I gained certification in my skills. When I used my intuition to do a reading. When I asked for higher powers to support me.

_____

2)

_____

3)

_____

4)

_____

5)

_____

6)

_____

7)

_____

8)

_____

9)

_____

10)

_____

Draw your idea of what this card looks like to you.

3. The Empress: Feminine and Feeling

3 - The Divine Woman	
Green Woman / Gaia / Mother / Empress	
You believe that all is connected and you have needed to care for others. Loving foundation.	Dreams of the mother energy are with you from long ago. Your mother is still an influence.
Great "feminine" energy recently. You may have had to support others or give tough love. Divine Mother!	You are the divine feminine personified. You walk in grace and beauty. Goddess. Caring, but strong.
You are either about to fall pregnant; or need to be caring and loving to others around you soon.	You have strong feminine (even from a man) support around you now. You are loved and encouraged.
Be caring and loving, and listen to others, but then act on what You think is right for all.	You're heading into the "mothering" energy. Caring for family; extended family or Earth.

The Empress, as it is known in the original tarot, is the Divine Woman or the Divine Mother. The Divine Woman can come up for either a male or a female in a reading as it indicates the beautiful, warm, loving and nurturing aspect of ourselves.

Some examples of what this card may mean when it comes up in a reading are below:

- Earth Mother; Gaia, and the need to protect the Earth.
- Pregnancy.
- A need to become a mother and/or to nurture others.
- The Goddess energy; being in your divine woman and admired by others.
- Motherhood.
- Becoming closer to nature.
- Becoming attractive to the opposite sex.
- If in the negative, this person may be a martyr, using the feminine energy incorrectly.
- Perhaps a need to be less giving of yourself and let people take care of themselves for a while. This is appropriate for those parents that give too much of themselves and are taken for granted.
- A need for tough love.

This card may show up if the person is a nurturer, or is blocking the mothering energy somehow.

Exercise: The Empress

Look at The Empress card again and this time think of your own life. Write down ten examples where you have had The Empress energy in your life.

1) Example: when I became a mother. When I decided to sell food for a living in my own cafe. When I made dresses for family. When I punished my son for bad behavior.

2)

3)

4)

5)

6)

7)

8)

9)

10)

Draw your idea of what this card looks like to you.

4. The Emperor: Masculine and Thinking

4 - The Divine Man Green Man / Father / Emperor	
You're usually in control and can provide food, shelter, clothing and love to others.	Dreams of the father energy are with you from long ago. Men from your past are impacting.
Great grounded energy recently. You may have had to be in control and lead others. You've shown strength.	You are the divine masculine now; "the boss". You're walking in your power try not to overpower others.
You need to be strong for everyone around you soon. Try and be gentle, but do what you need too.	You have strong masculine or father energy around you now. It may be from a strong and practical female.
Strength comes from the heart not from muscles. Use this strength now. Toughen up nicely.	You're heading into the "father" energy. Managing family, business, money. You'll be in control.

The Emperor, as it is known in the original tarot, is the Divine Man or the Divine Father. The Divine Man can come up for either a male or a female in a reading and indicates the fathering energy and aspect in all of us.

The Divine Man is also known as the Green Man who is the Earth Father, and the masculine equivalent of Gaia the Earth Mother.

Some examples of what this card may mean when it comes up in a reading are below:

- The Divine Man; a man put on a pedestal by others around him.
- A need to be in control, in charge, and managing others.
- A family owned business, and the management of this.
- A need to provide for, and protect others.
- The father and fatherhood.
- The fathering energy; looking after, protecting and loving family.
- Becoming closer to nature (the same as for The Divine Woman.)
- Becoming attractive to the opposite sex.
- If in the negative, this person may be a bully, using the masculine energy incorrectly.

This card may show up if the person is a controller and manager, or is blocking the positive aspects of the fathering energy somehow.

Exercise: The Emperor

Look at The Emperor card again and this time think of your own life. Write down ten examples where you have had The Emperor energy in your life.

1) Example: when I became a father. When I decided to own a cafe business. When I became aware that I was the boss of my own destiny.

_____

2)

_____

3)

_____

4)

_____

5)

_____

6)

_____

7)

_____

8)

_____

9)

_____

10)

_____

Draw your idea of what this card looks like to you.

5. The Hierophant: Tradition and Higher Authority

5 - The Hierophant	
The Traditional Approach / Spirituality	
You prefer to do everything in life the "right way"; with integrity and honour. Tradition.	You've tried to do everything the right way in the past and wanted to follow a traditional path.
Recently you've needed to be strong and practical and be true to what you believe is right.	You're trying to do everything the "right way" now. There may be large groups of people around you.
You're crossed by the need to have a belief in something bigger than yourself or a traditional career.	Your environment may feel solid and reassuring, or overwhelming. A large group is surrounding you.
You need to have faith in yourself, or move into a traditional career: teaching, health etc	Your future is safe, secure and connected to others; maybe even by marriage.

The Hierophant is the more traditional aspects of society, or that which is deep and meaningful for many people e.g., Christianity. If this card comes up when talking about a person, it indicates that the person likes to do everything the right way and is a traditionalist, as dictated by that person's perception of what normal and traditional actually is, remembering that across the world, the traditional way is very different culture to culture.

Some examples of what this card may mean when it comes up in a reading are below:

- A need to become more spiritual or a very spiritual person who has a solid faith and core belief system which makes them a valuable member of society.
- A person who has taken on a traditional role e.g., teacher, solicitor, health practitioner, priest etc. A health practitioner in the traditional sense can also mean a Shaman, a massage therapist, a naturopath, a herbalist, and all of those other traditional roles which have come forward from thousands of years ago.
- The traditional aspects of society e.g., education, health, religion, transport, defence and other large organisations within the culture of the person being read for.
- A large organisation or working for a large organization, not a family owned business.
- Large groups of people.
- A union in a traditional way e.g., Marriage.
- In the negative, this person may be stubborn and think that their way is the only right way of doing things and may be trying to get everyone around them to do things their way.

Exercise: The Hierophant

Look at The Hierophant card again and this time think of your own life. Write down ten examples where you have had The Hierophant energy in your life.

1) Example: when I chose to marry before having children. When I decided to make up my own religion and live by my own set of beliefs. When I got married. When I became a teacher, or took on another traditional role in society.

_____

2)

_____

3)

_____

4)

_____

5)

_____

6)

_____

7)

_____

8)

_____

9)

_____

10)

_____

Draw your idea of what this card looks like to you.

6. The Lovers: Soul Mate Relationships

6 - The Lovers
Soul Mate Relationships / Right Timing

You are here to create harmony amongst many people. You are usually balanced.	You've had a good (or horrible) soul mate relationship in the past which is remembered now.
You've had a recent experience which is perfect for your soul growth, with a person or your work.	You're in the right place, at the right time, with the right people. Hopefully it feels good and not a difficult trial.
There's tension around you from a person or your work. Soul growth needed now.	The people and place around you is right for you right now, even if it doesn't feel like it.
You've had a burning desire to do something and you're denying yourself. Life is meant to be lived.	Your current future is looking perfect for you, but may not be easy. A healing, loving, learning time soon.

Soul Mate relationships and right timing is indicated by this card. A soul mate relationship isn't necessarily pleasant, as it can often mean that something has happened in a past life (perhaps you killed someone) and in this lifetime, you've agree to come back together to learn how to be kind to each other. It's unusual for anyone to have children with a Soul Mate, as generally the lesson is learnt and the relationship is no longer required and people move on.

There are Soul Mate relationships whereby two people have agreed to come into this lifetime and just love and support each other, having children together and being kind to others around them, using their relationship as an example of how two people can give unconditional love to each other. These relationships are beautiful, but rare. A Soul Mate may be a child, a mother, a sibling, a friend or a loved pet.

Some examples of what this card may mean when it comes up in a reading are below:

- An actual loving Soul Mate relationship where you meet and want to share a lifetime together and feel that you know each other intimately after only a short time.
- A need for an in-depth conversation between couples to resolve long standing issues.
- A love triangle, whereby two people are in love with the same person.
- When around career, this card indicates right timing is playing a part in the events that are occurring. No matter how this actually feels to the person being read for, they may feel great at work, or horrible about what's happening, this card says you are in the right place at the right time.
- If the question is about the environment, then the same message applies, you are in the right place at the right time no matter how it actually feels.

Exercise: The Lovers

Look at The Lovers card again and this time think of your own life. Write down ten examples where you have had The Lovers energy in your life.

1) Example: when I went into relationship with my partner. When there was a love triangle and massive change around relationships. When I decided to have a baby and bring in another soul mate relationship.

   _____

2)

   _____

3)

   _____

4)

   _____

5)

   _____

6)

   _____

7)

   _____

8)

   _____

9)

   _____

10)

   _____

Draw your idea of what this card looks like to you.

7. The Chariot: Choices and Successful Endeavors

7 - The Chariot
Successful Completion / Support to Others

You are successful at anything you put your mind too and you tend to rescue other people.	You've had a past success which is on your mind now. You are reminded you are fabulous!
Recent movement and changes and successful completions of major life works. Well done!	You're expending a lot of energy now, which is alright as you seem to have an unlimited supply. Charge!
You're crossed by a fork in life's road. Either way you go will be successful, so choose calmly.	You're well supported by the people around you and your life/work environment.
If you've been stagnating because you're scared to pick a direction, then rest easy. All choices are right!	You're getting bigger, better and stronger every day. Life is becoming easy for you. You'll be successful.

If you find yourself at a crossroads, then this card shows you that whichever way you go, you will have a fabulous outcome. The Chariot generally means a good outcome for any question being asked. This card can also depict a person that swoops in and saves others.

People generally want a reading to see the outcome of moving in a particular direction in their lives e.g., do I stay or go in this relationship? Do I stay working where I am now, or do I take the other offer elsewhere? Do I stay in this town, or move?

If The Chariot has shown up, then you don't have to worry about the choices you need to make as either way will be successful. The message when this card shows up is always if you pick a path, it is the right path.

Some examples of what this card may mean when it comes up in a reading are below:

- Get the job done! Put in a lot of effort now and reap the rewards.
- Help other people as you have plenty of energy to give to others.
- Success at anything you care to do.
- It doesn't matter which way you go now, you will be successful either way.

Exercise: The Chariot

Look at The Chariot card again and this time think of your own life. Write down ten examples where you have had The Chariot energy in your life.

1) Example: when I realised I was in a fork in the road, but it didn't matter which way I went because it was all good. When I realized I was going to win, win, win! When I decided to go to the rescue of a friend.

_____

2)

_____

3)

_____

4)

_____

5)

_____

6)

_____

7)

_____

8)

_____

9)

_____

10)

_____

Draw your idea of what this card looks like to you.

51. Sample Question for Course

Natalie wants to know if it's possible to do well in her studies and draws The Magician card. What do you tell her?

    A. You'll do ok if you leave it up to spirit.

    B. There's not much to do, spirit is guiding you and supporting you.

    C. You are able to manifest now – so if you are studying, then you'll do well, and if you're not studying, then you won't do well. You reap what you sow with this card.

    D. None of the above.

52. 7. Sample Question for Course

Shae wants to connect more spiritually to life and asks for guidance, and draws The High Priestess. What do you tell her?

    A. This is the card of intuition and divine guidance. Sit in quiet meditation, or find a course of study which will open your intuition more. You will be guided by spirit.

    B. There's nothing to do except wait for spirit to help you.

    C. None of the above.

53. 9. Sample Question for Course

Natalie wants a farm to grow vegetables and have chickens. Which card best shows her alignment to the Earth?

    A. The Emperor.

    B. The Empress.

    C. The High Priestess.

    D. None of the above.

54. Sample Question for Course

Which definition best describes The Emperor?

    A. You're the boss.

    B. This is the divine man, father, and masculine card and reflects mental drive and an ability to manage.

    C. The ability to have children and manage family matters.

    D. None of the above.

The Mental Journey

Mental journey on Earth

This section is all about the mental processes that the soul lives through. We've already discussed building our own home, and a lot of what happens when building a home is physical, talking it through, understanding that we have to get on with others and actually doing things. We can continue to use the analogy of building a home when we talk about the mental journey.

Read through this example:

- **Decision and legal paperwork. "I'm so sick of paperwork!"** 8 – Justice: We need to put our plans in writing to prove our decisions are really what we've agreed upon. There's no point just chatting to someone in authority about your building plans and having them say "that sounds ok, go ahead with that," that would never happen. We have to put our plans into writing and then have those bits of paper approved.

- **Individuality. "So why do I have to conform?"** 9 – The Hermit: It can be hard to try and build a home in conjunction with a whole heap of approvals, and The Hermit does like to do things his/her own way. The lesson for us is that we still want to retain our individuality when we're building a home and we don't want to conform so much that we lose our identity, otherwise there'd be no architects in the world and everyone would live in the exact same structures. Although the end result is something that The Hermit craves, a little cave/home of their own where they can hide from the world, we need to learn to have our independence whilst working with others.

- **Opportunity. "I just discovered I can get a cheap water tank!"** 10 – **The Wheel of Fortune:** If we stay positive while building our home and talking to the people that we need to talk too, then we may discover new and exciting opportunities that we hadn't even considered before. The bank may tell you about a new type of home loan that is being trialed. A builder may remind you that bricks are cheaper this month. The council may let you know about a special offer for home builders in a certain area. If you're not open to talking to other people then you may miss a wonderful opportunity to do something even more special with your home.

- **Unlimited energy. "I can find the strength and time, I can!" 11 – Strength:** Sometimes we have to find the energy even when we're getting sick of a project. We might decide half way through building the house that we should never have started, and that the challenge is way too big and we're just over it and want it to end. Even when humans fight Gods in movies, the human has a way of winning and the challenge isn't a real one. Let's face it, a God could squash a human under one fingernail, but in the parables the human does get a chance to win out over the odds. There's always a way. Keep moving. You have the power and the energy to complete the projects.

- **Wisdom and lessons. "I can't believe we didn't get council approval!" 12 – The Hanged Man:** Sometimes we have to change plans because of things that happen outside of ourselves that we have no control over. Sometimes we can't hire the nail gun when we want too. Sometimes it rains when we had planned to paint the outside of the house. Sometimes we have to stop everything whilst we spend money on something that's come up that's more important. This too shall pass is a great mantra for this time in any major project. There's lots of things that happen that we can't control, so we may as well just get over it and get on with it.

- **Change. "Let's build an investment block of units instead." 13 – Death:** Sometimes there are life situations that cause us to stop what we're doing and change direction entirely. I know the Death card looks negative, but all tarot cards can be considered positive and negative. Imagine that you've just finished a meeting with the council and other regulatory people and they approve plans for your dream home. The next day you meet with your accountant and they strongly recommend that you build an investment property instead, maybe units! Argh! What to do. If you decide to change your plans in a radical way, then this can be indicated by the Death card. Sometimes bad things do happen. Someone has an accident and you decide to move towns to be closer to family and the house plans stop. Just remember that the Death card just means change. Abrupt and unwelcome, or planned and welcome.

- **Finding balance. "Let's build on Saturdays and take Sundays off!" 14 – Temperance:** If we become too unbalanced in one part of our life, then we can often become stressed and then unwell. We have to remember to have a life, and not be consumed by our projects. Sometimes it's more important for the long-term to take a break and figure out ways of achieving your home building goal in a way that's not going to stress everyone unduly.

As you can see, the mental process works in alignment with the physical process. You can't go and do things unless you've made a decision first.

8. Justice: Decisions and Legal Paperwork

8 - Justice	
Decisions / Legal Paperwork / Defence	
You are a decision maker who has a clear sense of right from wrong. Assist others with this.	Major decisions you've made from your past are on your mind now, and impacting you.
There's been a major decision making process recently take place. Hopefully this was pleasant for you.	You are in the decision maker role right now, or have a need to protect others around you. You are mighty!
Soon there will be big decisions to be made and perhaps legal paperwork to sign. Stay calm.	There are decisions that are being made by people around you; possibly legal.
You need to pull out your paperwork and check your contracts, as others around you are doing this now.	You are heading towards either a life changing decision, a need to defend others or there will be papers to sign.

There are always little decisions to be made. What do we have for lunch? Where will we go next? There is a seemingly endless list of decisions that we make over a lifetime.

This card doesn't indicate little decisions like what to cook for lunch. The Justice card indicates the much larger decisions in life. If your major life decisions are made by others, they may be made in a court of law and you may need to suffer the consequences of that decision.

Generally major life decisions are written down and signed, making the decisions legally binding. Therefore this card can indicate legal paperwork. It could the purchase of a house, a rental agreement, signing the contract in a new job, or getting a divorce for example. Whether the legal paperwork, or the life changing decision that needs to be made, feels good or bad is of no consequence with the Justice card. This card will show up if a major decision point in your life has now been reached.

If this card is describing who someone is, then that person has a justice theme in their lives and will no doubt make errors in judgement early in life to enable the lesson of right and wrong to be learnt. A person with a positive justice theme will be drawn to the right way of doing things in life and may have a desire to support and protect the innocent e.g., defence force, police force, or even work that has a set process and a set right way of doing things. A person with a negative justice theme may be drawn to a life of crime.

Some examples of what this card may mean when it comes up in a reading are below:

- Make a decision or other people will make it for you.
- Go into a career which serves and protects others, or has a distinct right way of doing things.
- Review carefully all paperwork and get it completed.
- There's legal paperwork to be signed.
- If in the negative, this could mean that you're making too many decisions for other people, and that you should step back and let other people make decisions for themselves.

Exercise: Justice

Look at your Justice card and think of your own life. Write down ten examples where you have had the justice energy in your life.

1) Example: when I wrote everything down as proof. When I went to court. When I signed legal paperwork. When I made a massive decision to go through with a divorce.

_____

2)

_____

3)

_____

4)

_____

5)

_____

6)

_____

7)

_____

8)

_____

9)

_____

10)

_____

Draw your idea of what this card looks like to you.

9. The Hermit: Individuality

<table>
<tr><td colspan="2" align="center">9 – The Hermit
The Druid / Inner Guidance / Isolation</td></tr>
<tr><td>You are the wise druid that needs to have isolation in order to recharge. Strong individual.</td><td>You remember a time when you had to rely on yourself alone. You are a strong individual.</td></tr>
<tr><td>You've recently had to think about your life without discussing it with others. You may have felt alone.</td><td>You have a lot of inner wisdom which can be shared. You do not need many people around you now.</td></tr>
<tr><td>You either feel sad and lonely, or need time alone now. Remember you are a strong person.</td><td>Your environment feels isolated, or you have peaceful and strong individuals around.</td></tr>
<tr><td>You need to make decisions using your inner wisdom and try not to rely on others to live your life for you.</td><td>You're going to be wandering away by yourself for a while. Even if just in your thoughts. Be the strong individual.</td></tr>
</table>

The Hermit is the person that relies on inner guidance. The Hermit is a person that is happy to be around other people, but may need quiet time in order to recharge and think things through.

The Hermit may need to wander off into the wilderness alone in order to contemplate the universe and their inner truth and knowledge.

Some examples of what this card may mean when it comes up in a reading are below:

- You need time alone to consider how you really feel about a situation, and what you really want to do next.
- You need to make up your own mind using the knowledge that you already have.
- You may be feeling lonely and it might be time for you to get out and meet new people.
- You have inner wisdom that you need to share with others now.
- If in the negative, you might feel that you know everything that you need to know, but you may be missing some important facts.

Exercise: The Hermit

Look at The Hermit card again and think of your own life. Write down ten examples where you have had The Hermit energy in your life.

1) Example: when I decided to wander off by myself for a while. When I realized that I loved other people's opinions, but I had to listen to my own inner guidance and follow my own direction.

_____

2)

_____

3)

_____

4)

_____

5)

_____

6)

_____

7)

_____

8)

_____

9)

_____

10)

_____

Draw your idea of what this card looks like to you.

10. The Wheel of Fortune: Opportunity

10 – The Wheel of Fortune
Fate / Opportunity / Changes

You are usually able to deal with the major changes in life and don't miss opportunities.	A life changing opportunity from your past is on your mind now. Did you take it or not?
You've had recent changes and are probably feeling like you're still spinning from them. Movement.	If life's good at the moment, enjoy it as it's about to change. If life's not good now, it will be, it's changing.
An opportunity is in front of you which may or may not feel comfortable. The wheel turns.	Your environment is changing and there are opportunities to improve it now.
It's about time you took a chance. Life doesn't give too many opportunities for great change, so don't miss out!	Your future shows continuing expansion. Karma is playing a hand in your future. What you do now counts!

If The Wheel of Fortune has rolled into your reading, then you are being told that there is opportunity around you and if you don't like your current situation, then it's going to be alright as it is changing. Conversely if you **do** like your current situation, then enjoy it, as it's also going to change.

The Wheel turns, if you don't take the opportunities presented to you, then you'll miss out.

Some examples of what this card may mean when it comes up in a reading are below:

- There are too many opportunities around you, too many choices for you to pick from.
- There is a fabulous opportunity that needs to be grabbed now.
- There are opportunities coming, keep looking!
- You might need to look around yourself and see what the world has to offer you.
- Fate and Karma might be showing in your life now. The Wheel reflects back to you those things that you have done in the past, the learning cycle and the cycle of life.

Exercise: The Wheel of Fortune

Look at The Wheel of Fortune card and think of your own life. Write down ten examples where you have had The Wheel of Fortune energy in your life.

1) Example: when I decided to leave my past behind and just go forward with a fresh start. When I was surrounded by work opportunities.

_____

2)

_____

3)

_____

4)

_____

5)

_____

6)

_____

7)

_____

8)

_____

9)

_____

10)

_____

Draw your idea of what this card looks like to you.

11. Strength: Unlimited Energy

11 – Strength	
Harnessing Universal Energy / Power	
You are usually strong enough to deal with whatever situation or event you or others have.	You've proven to yourself long ago that you are strong enough to deal with anything life gives.
You've recently had to show enormous strength. Not just for yourself, but for those around you.	You are incredibly brave and incredibly strong and are able to support and strengthen others.
You're being asked to step into your power soon. You can soon harness universal energy.	Your environment lends you great strength and support. Tough people near you.
You need to either change careers to be closer to nature, or you need to start gently standing up for yourself.	You're moving into a time where you will harness great amounts of passion and universal energy. Enjoy!

The Strength card always signifies harnessing universal energy, pulling the energy from around you and pushing it through you. People who can harness universal energy are usually very good with plants and animals as they can speak the same universal language as the elementals - those beings of nature - do.

Some examples of what this card may mean when it comes up in a reading are below:

- You are strong enough to help yourself and everyone around you.
- Just keep going, you're building and growing every day.
- You'll need enormous strength and endurance, and luckily you'll have it!
- Perhaps change your work to reflect something closer to nature, or a career in looking after animals.
- If in the negative, you may be overpowering others. Try and become gentler.

Exercise: Strength

Look at your Strength card again and this time think of your own life. Write down ten examples where you have had Strength energy in your life.

1) Example: when I realized how strong I was. When I decided to give my relationship another go and work harder. When I used my strength in support of children or animals.

_____

2)

_____

3)

_____

4)

_____

5)

_____

6)

_____

7)

_____

8)

_____

9)

_____

10)

_____

Draw your idea of what this card looks like to you.

12.   The Hanged Man: Wisdom and Lessons

12 – The Hanged Man	
Watch, Wait, Listen and Learn Something	
You understand that being patient is one of the greatest powers of mankind. All things change.	You've either been martyred in the past, or have learnt to think before making changes.
You've had a recent experience where you felt powerless to change anything. That's changing.	You can't change your situation right now. You have to learn, wait, watch and prepare until the time is right.
You need to come to a standstill whilst you or others around you make life decisions.	There's no way to change your environment or the people around you now. Be careful.
There's nothing you can do to change your situation. Be calm and meditate. Don't change anything.	You're heading towards a feeling of powerlessness. Take the advice in this reading to avert this outcome.

We all want to be wise, but the lessons can be painful. The energy of The Hanged Man is that of the Norse God Odin who hung himself from the tree of knowledge for nine days as he was promised the wisdom of the runes. You have to stop, wait, watch, listen and learn something now. You can't change your situation no matter how much you may want too or how unfair things may appear.

There is a karmic influence around now, and if something is happening without your permission or conscious understanding, then know that you are being instructed to use this time to learn and grow as a person. A debt that you're unaware of is being paid back now. Generally you can't change the circumstances, and that means that you have to change something else, probably your perception and beliefs.

Some examples of what this card may mean when it comes up in a reading are below:

- It's time for you to meditate and become more present in your everyday life. You are being challenged to find joy in those things that you usually find frustrating.
- You are being made the victim in a situation and cannot change anything about it. Just breath through it as life is changing and this circumstance will not last forever.
- You have to stop what you're doing and learn more before proceeding.
- You can't change your environment, your situation or the people around you. Don't bother trying. Just love people and events the way they are.
- You may be trying to do too much too soon. Slow down and make sure to check that you're heading the right direction.

Exercise: The Hanged Man

Look at The Hanged Man card again and this time think of your own life. Write down ten examples where you have had The Hanged Man energy in your life.

1) Example: when I realized that I had to wait a while before leaving a particular job. When I decided to stop moving forward and learn something special. When I was blamed for something I didn't do and I can't do anything about it.

_____

2)

_____

3)

_____

4)

_____

5)

_____

6)

_____

7)

_____

8)

_____

9)

_____

10)

_____

Draw your idea of what this card looks like to you.

13. Death: Change

13 - Change
Rebirth / Reincarnation / Endings

You cope well in the tough situations in life and are usually very good with change.	You remember a massive change that occurred in your past with joy or sadness.
You've recently had a major change take place. This may be happy or sad. A rebirth or reincarnation.	You're in the middle of a change right now that may feel good or bad. Life constantly changes. Accept it.
Too much change is causing you chaos at the moment. Stay focussed on reality.	There's massive change taking place around you now. Changes with friendships / lovers.
Move calmly into change now. Life is changing anyway, so there's no point in being worried about everything.	You're heading towards a time of rebirth. A new beginning. Set your life up the way you want and enjoy!

People are generally worried when this card shows up in a reading however, change is the only constant in life and therefore needs to be embraced. Like night and day, the rain before the sunshine, we need change in order to grow.

Some examples of what this card may mean when it comes up in a reading are below:

- The ending of a major life-cycle, and therefore the beginning of a new lifecycle. For instance, leaving a house/job/place in order to move to another house/job/place.
- Change is coming and change is around you. Try and enjoy it.
- If in the negative, there may be too many changes taking place causing chaos. Try and do changes in your life systematically, completing one thing before starting another.
- If the question is about an outcome, then this card does not bode well. This card says things will not end well unless something is done differently by the people involved.
- If the reading is about a house move, then de-clutter is the message from the Death card. Don't take the old with you into the new.

Exercise: Death

Look at the Death card again and this time think of your own life. Write down ten examples where you have had Death energy in your life.

1) Example: when I decided to clean out all the old rubbish that was cluttering up my home and had a garage sale. When I realized that the project would fail if I kept going in a particular direction. When my friend left without explaining to me why. When I realized that sometimes life does make changes without my permission.

_____

2)

_____

3)

_____

4)

_____

5)

_____

6)

_____

7)

_____

8)

_____

9)

_____

10)

_____

Draw your idea of what this card looks like to you.

14.   Temperance: Finding Balance

14 – Temperance
Maintain Balance / Medicines

You are very good at keeping your balance through major life changes. You heal well.	You remember a time in your past where you had to keep your balance through change.
You've recently had to keep your balance through a life experience which may have included healing.	You are going through changes now and need to keep calm, eat well and stay grounded to keep healthy.
Everything in moderation is a requirement for you and others around you now. Be calm.	There may be illness in your environment, or your friends may be having trouble.
You're mixing the medicine of your soul every time you eat or drink or exercise. Look after yourself.	Your future looks secure, as long as you keep a balanced approach to coming change and to your health.

Temperance will show up in a reading when you need to keep your balance through changes. This card can also indicate a need for medicines; herbal or scientific remedies to assist in the healing process.

You are mixing the medicine within your soul, growing and changing rapidly. Sometimes if the soul wants you to head in a different direction than your mind does, and you fight against your soul's direction continuously, illness can occur to make you stop and review your life, and hopefully force you to make the necessary changes to your current path.

Some examples of what this card may mean when it comes up in a reading are below:

- There are changes occurring in and around the body that require calm and steady process to avoid falling ill e.g., When you change jobs or homes, the stress can sometimes cause colds and the flu. Look after your health when undergoing changes.
- Medicines may be required to assist the health of the body right now.
- Stay calm when others around you are finding it difficult too.

Exercise: Temperance

Look at the Temperance card again and this time think of your own life. Write down ten examples where you have had Temperance energy in your life.

1) Example: when I couldn't quite figure out what to do and felt a little bit sick physically because I was so unsure. When I decided to maintain the harmony in my home regardless of what was happening. When I checked into hospital for the healing treatment.

2)

3)

4)

5)

6)

7)

8)

9)

10)

Draw your idea of what this card looks like to you.

55. Sample Question for Course

If The Death card is drawn in a reading when a person asks about changing jobs, what would you tell them?

A. This card indicates change is necessary.
B. This card can mean change is happening regardless of what you do.
C. This card indicates fast and fresh changes.
D. All of the above.

56. Sample Question for Course

The Hermit card is drawn as an outcome card for a person who is asking if they'll ever have a relationship. Which is the most right?

A. This card in the outcome position can mean that you are destined to be alone.
B. This card in the outcome position means that you have a strong personality and you like your space. It's a warning that if you don't open your heart and house to the possibility of love that it won't come to you.
C. This card in the outcome position means that you may end up alone if you keep going the way you are. Are you happy to share your home? Are you happy to share your wealth? Are you happy to share your heart? These are all questions that need to be answered to avert the outcome of walking alone. Let's look at the advice position for more information.
D. This card in the outcome position means that you're heading towards rethinking your living space and need to open up your home and heart before a partner can come into your life.

57. Sample Question for Course

If The Temperance card is drawn in a reading when a person asks about their health, what would you tell them?

A. You need balance in all things right now to maintain health.
B. This card can mean hospitals and ill health.
C. You are required to stay fit and healthy – get passionate about your health now before it's too late.
D. None of the above.

The Spiritual Journey

This section is all about the spiritual journey of being on the earth. We've already discussed building our own home, and a lot of what happens when building a home is mental and physical, thinking about things and then going ahead with them. We can continue to use the analogy of building a home when we talk about the spiritual journey.

Read through this example:

- **Contracts. "I can't believe I signed up for this!"** 15 – The Devil: We have to be so careful what we agree to do with our lifetime. If we choose to build a home it's a massive investment of our lifetime on Earth spent. Is it really part of your soul contract to build a house and learn about building a house? Or was it your driving passion on Earth to write a children's book which means you'd have to pay someone else to build your house? If you marry someone, you've gone into a soul contract. The marriage might be beautiful or horrible, but it's still a contract. We always have free will and therefore a choice. We can choose to enter any type of contract, which is why the phrase "the Devil is in the details" was created. It means that you have a choice, but once you agree, then you're committed to following through. We can overreact and break things and yell (acting devilishly,) but the same situation is still there when we calm down. We are free to break contracts, again we have free will and can choose freedom. We just have to be ready for the consequences of breaking the contract. We can't walk away from building a house without planning to do so.

- **Upheaval. "What do you mean a tree fell on our home?"** 16 – The **Tower:** This card is similar to the Death card in that people look at it and get a bit scared. It's not scary. The Tower signifies a massive event that's going to change things. The Tower could just mean that you're building a house and your environment is going to change when you move into it. The Tower can also mean that you find out that your accountant is a liar and has run off with all your money that you were using to build the house, and you've just found this out. The Tower signifies the roller coaster ride which is life and how we have to try and be serene whilst meeting the challenges that come because we planned them (we choose to move) or we didn't plan them (the dodgy accountant.) We need to try and plan everything, but sometimes plans have to change.

- **Hope. "Let's remember why we wanted to build this house." 17 – The Star:** We need to stay hopeful and keep focused on what we were hoping for when we first started on the journey of building the home. We have to remind ourselves of the enormous gifts that we have in our lives, where we have enough money to build a home, while others in the world have little. This isn't about feeling guilty for having too much. This is about being grateful for the wonderful gifts that have been bestowed upon you this lifetime. You chose to have a lifetime where you would have enough money to build your dream home.

- **Confusion and wishful thinking. "I'm confused." 18 – The Moon:** The moon is a dreaming card and all dreams can become unclear and unfocused when we awaken. Try and remember that like a dream, you have to write down your home plans so that you don't forget them later. This can be important with things like budgets. We may dream of having a spa bath in our back yard, but it might be just wishful thinking if we can't afford it. Remember to dream though, otherwise you might miss an idea that spirit is passing to you.

- **Warmth. "I'm so enjoying working with you, darling." 19 – The Sun:** The Moon can be dreamy and confusing, however The Sun can show things up in the cold and hard light of the day. The Sun is a positive and happy card which shows up flaws in the plan in a way that makes it easy for everyone. The Sun can come out when we've been worrying over an issue and finally realize that there's an easy way to do things. Warmth, teamwork and joy are all indicated and it can show that everyone's working happily together and that there'll be good outcomes.

- **Reward or punishment. "We got the house we planned to get." 20 – Judgment:** So how well did you plan the house? On building it have you discovered that you miscalculated on your building plans and made all the bedrooms too small to be useful? Is the house fabulous because of all the effort you put in? This card can indicate that you get out what you put in. It's the gateway to heaven or hell. A heaven or hell that we created ourselves.

- **Success and expansion. "We finished! Let's build another one!" 21 – The World:** Finally, we've made it. Yes, The Chariot can show us that we've successfully completed projects, but The World is the ultimate completion card. You may decide to open a building advice service for other people who want to build their own home, using all of the knowledge that you've attained over the course of building your own home. It's time now for you to enjoy the massive journey you've undertaken and consider using that knowledge and wisdom for your next adventure.

15. The Devil: Contracts

15 – The Devil	
Contracts / Marriage / Passion	
You take your commitments very seriously and try very hard to keep promises. You're passionate.	You've learnt that overreacting never helps yourself or others. A soul contract from long ago impacting now.
You've had a recent passionate experience, or entered a contract which hopefully you checked.	You're committed to the situation you are in, (work/love?) and are trying not to overreact to every situation.
You're about to enter a contract or have a passionate encounter. Think!	You're tied to the events around you and may or may not feel trapped.
You're taking no risks at all and need too, or you're being too risky and need to think things through right now!	You're heading towards a contract soon; e.g. a new relationship, a job, or other paperwork. Act after thinking.

The Devil appears when you're embarking on, or currently impacted by a contract with another person. As always, the devil's in the details with any contract, whether it's a physical contract that you have to sign, or a relationship contract which you are setting up or have to live with. We enter contracts all of the time:

- With another person that we come into a relationship with, a soul contract on how we want the relationship to be set up.
- With a child, if we bring a child into this earth we are binding ourselves to this little person until our end of the deal is complete.
- When we enter a job we usually sign a contract with the person we work for.
- When we buy or sell a house, car or other objects we also sign a contract.

Contracts are neither good nor bad, however they can certainly feel good or bad, and if we don't check the contract well, and set it up properly It can certainly make us suffer later.

For instance, consider this situation: You are going out to dinner because it's your mum's birthday. You could feel happy to be around your family, or you could feel trapped and horrible as you don't want to be around your family, but you have to be because it's your mum's birthday. The relationship contract is the same, it's just the way that you feel about it that makes it good or bad.

When you enter a relationship contract be careful how you set it up as you are creating the relationship contract by your behaviour.

The Devil showing up in a reading can also indicate that there is too much passion or energy around the person now and they need to be careful how they react.

Some examples of what this card may mean when it comes up in a reading are below:

- You are in a relationship contract, for good or bad.
- You are about to sign a contract and need to be mindful and check the details.
- You have too much passion right now and need to be careful of how you're reacting to situations. You may be over reacting to everything right now.
- You may also be taking no risks at all, and The Devil showing up as advice in your reading could indicate that you need to start looking at how you live your life and to maybe take some risks.

Exercise: The Devil

Look at The Devil card again and this time think of your own life. Write down ten examples where you have had The Devil energy in your life.

1) Example: when I signed the contract. When I got married. When I bought/sold a car/ house. When I over-reacted to everything.

_____

2)

_____

3)

_____

4)

_____

5)

_____

6)

_____

7)

_____

8)

_____

9)

_____

10)

_____

Draw your idea of what this card looks like to you.

16. The Tower: Upheaval

The Tower can be the scary card in the deck as it means major change and chaos. The three major changes that a person can go through apart from death and birth are: marriage, moving house, changing jobs, and divorce.

The Tower can indicate one of these major changes, or it can indicate that the person feels like they're living a life of chaos at the moment and that they need to clean up their lives and make their lives more calm again.

Some examples of what this card may mean when it comes up in a reading are below:

- House moves/job changes/births/deaths/marriages, any major change that can cause people to wobble a little.
- The need to make a major change.
- Everything around you is changing for the better or worse.

Exercise: The Tower

Look at The Tower card again and this time think of your own life. Write down ten examples where you have had The Tower energy in your life.

1) Example: when I moved. When I renovated my home. When the truth came out about the affair that I was trying to hide. When that person had to pay for their crime.

_____

2)

_____

3)

_____

4)

_____

5)

_____

6)

_____

7)

_____

8)

_____

9)

_____

10)

_____

Draw your idea of what this card looks like to you.

17. The Star: Hope

17 – The Star	
Gifts from Heaven / Hope / Wishes Granted	
You're usually the person that gives hope and comfort to others. You are a gift from heaven!	You've learnt that people only ever get those things they've asked for. Good or bad.
There's a feeling of connection to a higher power which has recently occurred filling you with hope and joy.	You're in a blessed situation now with gifts of many kinds being bestowed upon you. Ask for what you need.
You have free will and need to ask for what you wish for soon. Hope and joy coming. Manifest!	Your environment is filled with the opportunity to connect more with a higher power.
You need to ask for what you need, but not necessarily out loud. Be grateful for your life and ask with trust.	Your current future looks bright and joyful filled with everything you could possibly wish for. Wonderful!

The Star always means hope. There is no negative aspect to this card. You can wish upon a star. This card is confirmation that spirit has been listening to your prayers. This is the card of heaven's help.

Some examples of what this card may mean when it comes up in a reading are below:

- You are in contact with heaven, ask for what you want.
- What do you wish for? Ask for it and you will receive it if it's right for you.
- People in heaven are looking after you and guiding you.
- You are a hopeful person and are here to bring light to others.
- Your environment is wonderful and bright and promising.

Exercise: The Star

Look at The Star card again and this time think of your own life. Write down ten examples where you have had The Star energy in your life.

1) Example: the day I woke up and felt hopeful and happy for absolutely no reason. When I sat and did my vision board. When I did some wishing.

_____

2)

_____

3)

_____

4)

_____

5)

_____

6)

_____

7)

_____

8)

_____

9)

_____

10)

_____

Draw your idea of what this card looks like to you.

18. The Moon: Confusion and Wishful Thinking

18 – The Moon
Day Dreams and Wishful Thinking

You've always been a dreamer and are usually very creative, generous and kind.	There was a time long ago which is on your mind. Don't get lost in the dreams of the past.
Recent day dreaming and wishful thinking is impacting you now. You're not sure if events were real.	You have an opportunity to connect with a higher power whilst seeking clarity and staying grounded.
It's difficult to see clearly enough to make decisions. Can you wait before doing so?	There are dreams clouding your environment. It's difficult to see what's around you.
It may be time for you to start day dreaming about what your perfect life would be like. Meditate for clarity.	Your future is clouded by dreams. There's too much changing now. No clear outcome available.

The Moon can show up in a reading when there is a lot of wishful thinking and a need to communicate with spirit. Dreams are good for us, they allow us to grow and expand out of our current situation. However, when dreaming is all that's ever done, and no action is put behind those dreams, this can mean that people are asleep.

Some examples of what this card may mean when it comes up in a reading are below:

- The Divine Feminine, emotions and joyfulness.
- Meditation and a need to connect with spirit. This is doubly powerful if The High Priestess is also present in the reading.
- By the light of the silvery moon, all may not be as it appears.
- The way is clouded.
- You're not meant to know where you're heading yet as there is too much wishful thinking and the way is not clear.
- You may need to wake up from the dreams and actually do something, or conversely, you may need to do some wishful thinking and daydream about what your life might be like if you could wish for anything you want.

Exercise: The Moon

Look at The Moon card again and this time think of your own life. Write down ten examples where you have had The Moon energy in your life.

1) Example: when I realized I was unhappy with my work. When I was dreaming about a better future.

_____

2)

_____

3)

_____

4)

_____

5)

_____

6)

_____

7)

_____

8)

_____

9)

_____

10)

_____

Draw your idea of what this card looks like to you.

19. The Sun: Warmth

19 – The Sun	
Warmth / Love / Friendship / Teamwork	
You are a sunny person who usually attracts people. You bring warmth and love to others.	You have beautiful memories which fill you with light. You understand the power of warmth.
There's been a recent experience where "the sun has come out" and shined happy light on your life.	Love, friendship, teamwork, joyfulness. Life's good and don't you know it? Expand and fly high!
If times have been hard, don't worry, the sun is coming out and all will feel fabulous soon.	Your life must be feeling warm and loving now with all of the right people around you.
Don't block yourself, you have the power of the sun within you and it will hurt to deny yourself. Act now!	Wow! Your future is looking fabulous; love, warmth and happiness all coming to you. Enjoy! Well done!

The Sun is warmth, love, camaraderie, friendship, union, joyfulness. Everything that's warm, sunny, joyful and happy. To me the Sun is the second best card in the deck and indicates that all is well and that relationships are blossoming.

Some examples of what this card may mean when it comes up in a reading are below:

- The sun is coming out. If you've had a hard time and the sun is present in your reading, then everything will turn out well for everyone.
- The people around you are wonderful.
- Your environment and your work are great.
- Life is good and you can give some of your warmth to others now.

Exercise: The Sun

Look at The Sun card again and this time think of your own life. Write down ten examples where you have had The Sun energy in your life.

1) Example: when I realized that my relationships were just perfect as they were. When I wanted to move closer to the beach/coast/sunshine. When I met that person for the first time. When I finally saw my situation in a really clear light.

_____

2)

_____

3)

_____

4)

_____

5)

_____

6)

_____

7)

_____

8)

_____

9)

_____

10)

_____

Draw your idea of what this card looks like to you.

20. Judgment: Reward or Punishment

20 – Judgement
Self Perception / Major Life Choices / Rebirth

You've always been the kind of person that can make massive changes easily.	A big decision from your past is impacting you now. If good, remember. If bad, learn from it.
There's been a recent decision which impacts everything in your life. Hopefully it was your decision.	This is a time of judgement. Make sure you don't judge yourself harshly or others will too. Be gentle.
There's about to be a life changing decision made. Stay calm and support others.	You're looking at your environment considering changing it, or others are.
Stop judging yourself so harshly. You deserve good things to happen to you and don't need to be the martyr.	You're heading towards a major decision point. Start thinking now before others get to choose your life.

The Judgment card shows up in readings when a major decision is being made. It's similar to the Justice card in that regard, so if they're both present in your reading, then there are major decisions to be made and legal paperwork to sign in relation to the decision making process.

With the Judgment card by itself though, you're being judged by the hardest person there is - yourself. How do you feel about what you're doing in life? Do you feel good about yourself? Any feeling you have about yourself is being reflected back to you from others now. If you feel good about yourselves, then positive people will be around you. If you feel badly about yourself, then negative people will be attracted to you. Judgment is always about self-perception. Some examples of what this card may mean when it comes up in a reading are below:

- A big decision needs to be made now.
- You need to review the way you feel about yourself, as others are reflecting your own emotions back to you.
- This card reminds you that you deserve good things and if you don't believe you do, then that's why you're not getting them.

Exercise:

Look at your Judgment card again and this time think of your own life. Write down ten examples where you have had judgment energy in your life.

1) e.g., when I decided to leave my home town. When I decided which career path to take. When I decided that I would leave my partner.

_____

2)

_____

3)

_____

4)

_____

5)

_____

6)

_____

7)

_____

8)

_____

9)

_____

10)

_____

Draw your idea of what this card looks like to you.

21. The World: Success and Expansion

The World is the end of a major life cycle. This is the best card in the deck and when it shows up in a reading, there is no down side to your reading. Everything is going to turn out the best possible way for everyone involved.

As The World indicates success and happiness, it also means the dissolving of all boundaries. There are no restrictions to anything that you wish to do right now. You've learnt some amazing lessons, and you can use the journey that you've been on to your greatest benefit.

Some examples of what this card may mean when it comes up in a reading are below:

- You can use your expanded knowledge and learned wisdom to start a business.
- You can consider using your life's lessons to embark on a new career.
- The World is laid at your feet. You can travel the world, experience wonderful things and have great joy.
- The end of a major life cycle and a celebration of a job done well.
- Best possible outcome for everyone.
- Celebrate!
- Start considering what next to do with yourself. Now might be the time to consider a fresh start, in the same place, or elsewhere, or even starting a new cycle by learning something new.

Exercise: The World

Look at The World card and think of your own life. Write down ten examples where you have had The World energy in your life.

1) Example: when I travelled overseas. When I felt that I had completed my goals for fitness. When I realized that life was perfect and I could do anything and go anywhere.

_____

2)

_____

3)

_____

4)

_____

5)

_____

6)

_____

7)

_____

8)

_____

9)

_____

10)

_____

Draw your idea of what this card looks like to you.

58. Sample Question for Course

The Devil card is drawn around a work question. What do you say?

    A. There are people around you that you can't trust.

    B. There are contracts – both personal and in writing around you now.

    C. There may be a need to be careful what you say as this card can indicate passionate outbursts. It can also indicate signing contracts – and if you are, make sure you're checking all the details *before* you sign.

    D. You'll be very messy and emotional and have trouble being sensible.

59. Sample Question for Course

Ken asks about his work and what he should do to make it better and draws The Moon card. What do you tell him?

    This card is confusing – we need more cards to help us.

    A. This card can mean dissatisfaction and wishful thinking – we need another card to help us.

    B. This card indicates that nothing will change by wishing for it, but does caution you to make any changes carefully as the outcome isn't clear at this stage. We might need another couple of cards to help understand better what is happening at your work.

    C. You don't like the job and are being told in your dreams to quite immediately and go and find your dream role.

60. Sample Question for Course

Sally has planned to move to a new country and The Tower and The World both appear in her reading in the happening next and outcome spaces. What do you tell her?

    A. Wow! If looks like change is happening for you and you will love it.

    B. It appears you can have the changes you want.

    C. The Tower can indicate home and job changes as it shows the destruction of current foundations, and The World is the best card in the deck and means that the world is open and available to you. Everything looks wonderful for you continuing your plans to move overseas.

    D. All of the above are accurate.

CHAPTER TEN

Creating your own tarot card spread

When tarot cards are placed in a certain order on the table, this is called a reading card spread, or a card layout. The Celtic cross layout is one of the most common and popular. To do the Celtic cross spread layout ten cards are drawn and placed one after the other in order to reflect what each card means in that placement. Each different card position is called a situation, as each position relates to something that is happening now.

   This is the Celtic cross layout:

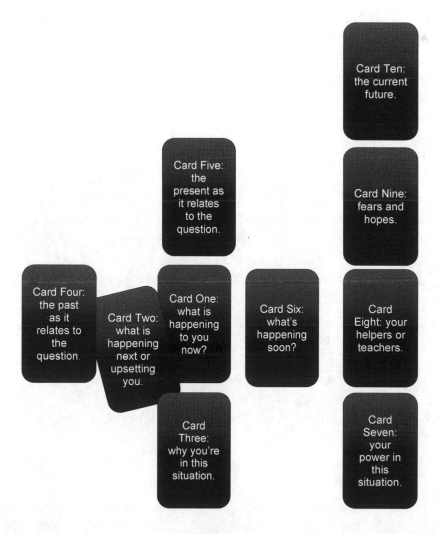

A simple card layout is the past, present and future spread. In this spread three cards are drawn randomly from the deck and placed face down in the past, present and future situations. Each card is then read in turn to see what the past, present and future hold.

Generally when people open a tarot deck for the first time, they have to look at the meaning of the card in a booklet, then they have to flip over to the page which shows what that spread's situation means e.g., past, and then they have to try and relate what that actual card means if placed in the past, as opposed to placing it in the present.

It's often easier when I'm doing a reading for someone to make up what I want the cards to mean as I'm doing the reading. For instance, a person may say that they are looking for a new job and I might think to myself: I shall ask for three cards, the first card will show me what their challenges are, the second card is their chances of success, and the third card will be a timeframe.

The important thing to remember when creating your spread is that **every place** in the spread relates to **right now.**

Say you did a reading for yourself as you are in relationship, and you decided in advance that you'd draw five cards. First card would be very distant past, second card would be distant past. When you draw those cards, then you have to understand that they're showing up in the reading because it might be something that happened a long time ago, but it's still impacting you **now**.

Many people make the mistake of thinking that if something happened in the past, then it doesn't impact them now, but if we haven't healed from an old breakup, then of course it may be impacting a current relationship.

If you pulled out three cards for your relationship and decided in advance that the cards meant past, present, and future and the first card was the Hermit, the second card was The Lovers, and the third card was Justice, then it might be saying that you learnt how to be a loner a long time ago, and you're undergoing soul growth with this partner which can be quite hard work, but your desire to be alone will probably mean you may push the relationship to a divorce.

| Card One
The Past

The Hermit | Card Two
The Present

The Lovers | Card Three
The Future

Justice |

The power is always ***right now*** and therefore you can never say that a reading has a definite future. You can certainly say that you are seeing a potential future if you keep going the way that you are, but it's not a definite future if you decide to change your hermit ways and adopt a better relationship mindset.

In this instance, if you pulled out one card for advice and it was the Three of Swords, then help from outside the relationship is needed to resolve the issues now! Or if the advice was the Four of Staves, then the message is to go somewhere romantic together, maybe a second honeymoon.

So as you can see from the above examples, you are allowed to make up your own spread. One that makes sense to you. If you make it up yourself, then you won't be confused by spread layouts that other people have created.

One of the most powerful spreads that I use is to draw three cards:

- First card: what mindset I should have in this situation?
- Second card: what I should actually ***do*** in this situation
- Third card: what am I forgetting in this situation?

Exercise:

Jenny decides to do a three-card reading, using the past, present and future spread and asks a question around her job security. Jenny draws the following cards:

The Knight of Pentacles is in the past. That means that Jenny may have undergone a recent change in job that is **still impacting her now**. If a job change in the past is still impacting Jenny now, then it's not surprising that any instability in her current role will be frightening.

The Death card showing in the present space can indicate that the job is not very stable and that Jenny may need to look around herself for another role very soon.

The Two of Staves in the future space is great, as it shows that Jenny will be making a decision around her job herself, rather than it being made for her. Simply by doing this reading for Jenny may be enough for her to have the courage to go looking for another job and then be in the position to choose between roles as is indicated by the Two of Staves.

Now draw out three cards for yourself and ask a question relevant to your life situation.

Below is the tarot card spread which I patented so that you can get an idea of a type of spread you can create for yourself.

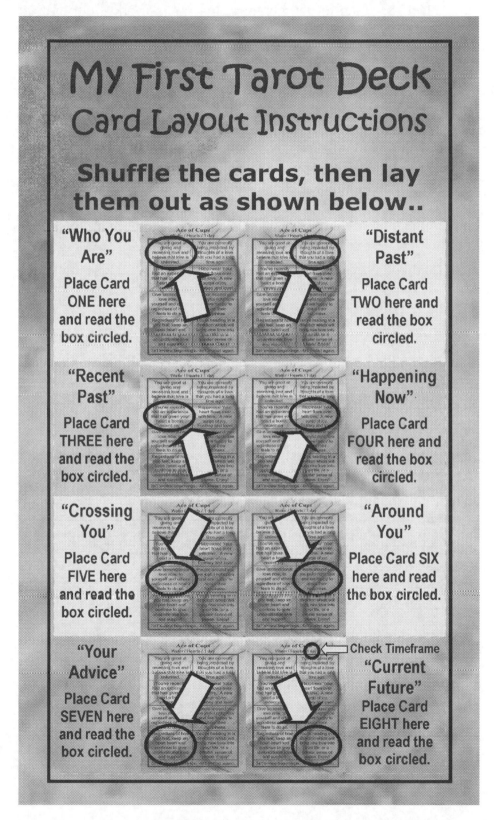

Well Done!

Thank you for taking the time to get this far in the coursework. I congratulate you on working through to this point and hope you aren't reading this on the first 'flick through' whilst still deciding whether or not you wish to purchase this book in a shop. ☺

A lot of people will be asking "what's next?"

I am offering anyone who submits their work to me, a certificate of completion which will assist you in gaining the confidence of your clients when doing a reading for them.

I am also offering an online course which is due by the end of 2015. Anyone who has done this coursework will simply need to do the online questions and submit the work online to become one of my accredited tarot practitioners.

Please, stay in touch and many blessings to you:

Eleanor Hammond MM

Answers to Sample Questions

1. Answer
Janie wants to know if she'd be happy in a new job and she's drawn a cups/water card from the deck. What do you tell her? B is correct.

2. Answer
Janie wants to know if she'd be happy in a new job and she's pulled out an air/swords card. What do you tell her? D is correct.

3. Answer
Which of the below is most right. Janie wants to know if she'd be happy in a new job and she's pulled out five cards; one from each of the five suits. A is correct.

4. Answer
Janie wants to fall pregnant and when you ask her to draw a card of her chances, you get the Ace of Swords, what do you tell her? B is correct.

5. Answer
Janie wants to fall pregnant and when you ask her to draw a card to see what her chances of falling pregnant are, she pulls out the Ace of Cups. What do you tell her? B is correct.

6. Answer
Janie wants to start a new business and when you ask her to draw three cards, she pulls out a heap of cards, all cups and swords. What do you tell her? D is correct.

7. Answer
Janie wants to know what she has to do in order to get a job and you ask the question for her and draw one card. The card is a Numbers card, what do you tell her? C is correct.

8. Answer
Janie wants to know what she has to do in order to get a job and you ask the question for her and draw one card. The card is a Court card, what do you tell her? B is correct.

9. Answer

Janie wants to know what she has to do in order to get a job and you ask the question for her and draw one card. The card is a Spirit card, what do you tell her? A is correct.

10. Answer

Janie has received a Spirit card on asking her question about what she has to do in order to get a job. Does that mean that she can relax and wait for things to happen? B is correct.

11. Answer

Janie has asked for a time frame around getting a job, what do you tell her? A is correct.

12. Answer

Janie has asked for a time frame around getting a job, and has pulled out one card which is the Two of Pentacles, what do you tell her? C is correct.

13. Answer

Which of the below answers is the 'most' right.
Janie has asked if time frames are accurate when asking the tarot cards. A is correct.

14. Answer

Janie has asked a time frame question and pulled out the Five of Staves. What time frame is this? A is correct.

15. Answer

Janie has asked a time frame question and pulled out the Ace of Pentacles. What time frame is this? D is correct.

16. Answer

Janie has asked a time frame question and pulled out The Chariot Major Arcana card. What time frame is this? D is correct.

17. Answer

Janie has asked how many weeks until she sees her family again and pulls out a spirit card. Which is the answer to give to Janie? D is most correct, however this is a spirit card. There really is no timeframe.

18. Answer

Jenny has asked for the name of the person who she is to meet this year and you draw three cards on her behalf and draw out two aces and a king. What do you tell her? C is correct.

19. Answer

You are doing a reading for Fran and you draw seven cards. You notice that the Three of Staves is the first card, and the Four of Staves is the seventh card pulled out. Do you mention a birth month to her? B is correct.

20. Answer

You do a reading for Janie and you have five cards on the table. There are three cups cards, all three in a row. The ace, two and three of cups are all in Janie's reading. Do you mention a birth month? D is correct.

21. Answer

Alyson asks if her relationship will last and you draw a card on her behalf whilst asking the question "can I have a yes/no answer please spirit around this question" and the card drawn is an even card. What do you say? Both A and C are correct.

22. Answer

Luke wants to figure out the best career that he could possibly do right now and you ask him to draw out a card and it's the Two of Swords. What do you tell him? D is correct.

23. Answer

Luke wants to know if a relationship will work out and you ask him to draw a card and he draws the Two of Cups. What do you tell him? B is correct.

24. Answer

Luke asks if he should stay in the same job that he's in now and pulls out three card. All of them are twos. The Two of Cups, the Two of Staves, and the Two of Swords. What do you tell him? D is correct.

25. Answer

Andrew says he isn't doing well at work and wants to know how his boss feels about him. He draws the Three of Staves. What do you tell him? C is right.

26. Answer

Andrew asks for a future reading and the Three of Swords is showing in the happening next position in the reading. What do you say about that? D is correct.

27. Answer

Bernadette has a health scare and is asking if she will be ok. The Four of Swords is drawn. What do you tell her? D is correct.

28. Answer

Bernadette is confused about a relationship and draws the Four of Cups. What do you tell her? D is correct.

29. Answer

Ken asks about his work and whether he should stay in his current role or move to another role. He draws the Five of Swords. Both answers below are right, which one is the *most* right? B is correct.

30. Answer

Ken wants to know what's happening with his friendship circle and he draws three cards, all fives. What do you tell him? C is correct.

31. Answer

Kate wants to go into a festival and compete to be the festival queen. You ask what her chances of becoming queen of the festival are, and ask Kate to draw one card. The card is the Six of Staves. What do you tell her? A is correct.

32. Answer

Kate said she'd like to meet someone and draws the Six of Cups. What do you tell her? A is correct.

33. Answer

Sarah wants to know if she'd be successful with her new job and she pulls out the Seven of Pentacles. What do you tell her? C is correct.

34. Answer

Sarah wants to travel and have fun, but people are telling her to apply for work. Sarah draws the Seven of Staves card. What do you tell her? D is correct.

35. Answer

Francis wants to work on her own and build a business and one of the cards drawn in the outcome space is the Eight of Pentacles. What do you tell her? C is correct.

36. Answer

Francis draws four cards, all of them eights. What do you tell her? D is correct.

37. Answer

Louise asks if she'll ever have any windfalls, and draws the Nine of Pentacles. What do you tell her? C is correct.

38. Answer

Louise doesn't understand why she feels so sad all of the time and draws the Nine of Staves out of the deck. What do you tell her? D is correct.

39. Answer

If someone asked a question around whether or not their relationship would be happy, drew out one card and it was the Ten of Cups, what would you tell them? C is correct.

40. Answer

Ronan asks if he'll be happy and draws the Ten of Staves. What do you tell him? C is correct.

41. Answer

Jenny wants to know if she is pregnant with a boy or a girl, what do you tell her when she draws the Page of Swords? B is correct.

42. Answer

Natasha wants to know how to handle a situation at work and draws the King of Swords. What do you tell her? D is correct.

43. Answer

Jane asks a question about a friend of hers and draws the Page of Swords card. What do you tell her? C is correct.

44. Answer

Jane wants to know how long it will be before she buys a house, and draws the Page of Pentacles. What do you tell her? C is correct.

45. Answer

The Knight of Pentacles is drawn in a reading and placed in the environment space. What do you tell the person? A is correct.

46. Answer

Three knights are showing in a reading. What do you say? D is correct.

47. Answer

Work has been difficult for Henry and he wants to change his career. He draws out the Queen of Pentacles. Which of the below is most right? B is correct.

48. Answer

Karen feels unhappy with the people around herself and asks what she needs to do to help relationships. The Queen of Cups is drawn. What do you tell her? A is correct.

49. Answer

Ken wants to know if he'll ever have a family and draws three kings. What do you tell him? D is correct.

50. Answer

Ken wants to know if he'll ever have a family and draws the King of Cups. What do you tell him? B is correct.

51. Answer

Natalie wants to know if it's possible to do well in her studies and draws The Magician card. What do you tell her? C is correct.

52. Answer

Shae wants to connect more spiritually to life and asks for guidance, and draws The High Priestess. What do you tell her? A is correct.

53. Answer

Natalie wants a farm to grow vegetables and have chickens. Which card best shows her alignment to the Earth? B is correct – as the Empress is often known as the Earth mother or Gaia card.

54. Answer

Which definition best describes The Emperor? B is correct.

55. Answer

If The Death card is drawn in a reading when a person asks about changing jobs, what would you tell them? D is correct.

56. Answer

The Hermit card is drawn as an outcome card for a person who is asking if they'll ever have a relationship. Which is the most right? C is correct.

57. Answer

If The Temperance card is drawn in a reading when a person asks about their health, what would you tell them? A is correct.

58. Answer

The Devil card is drawn around a work question. What do you say? C is correct.

59. Answer

Ken asks about his work and what he should do to make it better and draws The Moon card. What do you tell him? C is correct.

60. Answer

Sally has planned to move to a new country and The Tower and The World both appear in her reading in the happening next and outcome spaces. What do you tell her? D is correct.

About the Author

I am happily married and have three children and currently live in Mount Isa, central Queensland Australia.

I have always been focused on empowering others. In any role I've ever had, I've always wanted anyone coming into contact with me to be better after knowing me, than they were when I met them. I've done this through having employees that I've trained, and I endeavor to empower through readings by giving people the knowledge of how to help themselves through their life challenges.

My background as written by a journalist:

Eleanor has an interesting mix of bloodlines, and as a sixth generation Romany gypsy, Eleanor has dreamt of the original tarot cards all of her life. As a child Eleanor was given the Jack of Spades in a dream and told that this is your life purpose and that she needed to communicate that which is hidden.

Since then Eleanor has given tens of thousands of tarot readings over decades, and conducted energy work of all kinds, including Shamanic work becoming popular and sought after in the past decade in Australia.

Eleanor has been a successful and gentle group leader and teacher for tarot courses and other healing work.

Eleanor has a Master degree in Metaphysics (MM) and is a Reverend in the Universal Church of Metaphysical Sciences, using the Reverend title rarely as Eleanor does not believe in categorizations for their sake alone, preferring to call herself a shaman as this title appears to extend past a traditional boundary for most people.

Connect personally at:
www.facebook.com/EleanorEnergyHammond
www.eleanorhammond.com.au
eleanors.energy@gmail.com